# HEAVEN IN OUR HANDS

# Heaven in Our Hands

## Receiving the Blessings
## We Long For

### Fr. Benedict J. Groeschel, C.F.R.

CHARIS

Servant Publications
Ann Arbor, Michigan

Charis Books is an imprint of Servant Publications
especially designed to serve Roman Catholics.

Published by Servant Publications
P.O. Box 8617
Ann Arbor, Michigan 48107

Scripture texts in this work are taken from The Holy Bible, Revised Standard Version, Catholic Edition, copyright 1966 by the Division of Christian Education of the National Council of the Churches of Christ in the United States of America.

Cover design by Paula Murphy, Hile Design and Illustration

95 96 97 98 10 9 8 7 6 5 4

Printed in the United States of America
ISBN 0-89283-813-2

### Library of Congress Cataloging-in-Publication Data

Groeschel, Benedict J.
    Heaven in our hands : receiving the blessings we long for /
Benedict J. Groeschel.
        p.   cm.
    Includes bibliographical references.
    ISBN 0-89283-813-2
    1. Beatitudes.   2. Christian life–Catholic authors.   I Title.
BT382.G76  1994
241.5'3–dc20                                     94-26534
                                                      CIP

# *Dedication*

To all my friends on the West Coast
of the United States
who have prayerfully and graciously
encouraged me for so many years
and in so many ways.

# Contents

# Preface

*L*ike my previous book, *Healing the Original Wound,* this collection of conferences is presented at the request and with the support of Servant Publications and with the help of David Came, Heidi Hess, and especially of Pam Moran. I am deeply grateful. These talks on the Beatitudes were given originally in 1983 as part of my work as Director of the Office of Spiritual Development of the Archdiocese of New York. They have been completely revised and updated for this book, since the specific issues and examples have changed over the course of the decade; the timeless truth of the Sermon on the Mount, however, remains unaltered and undiluted. I hope and pray that each reader will clearly discern the call of the Holy Spirit in these chapters. I have tried to honestly present his invitations to all of the disciples of Our Lord Jesus Christ as best as my limitations allow.

I am particularly indebted to my two friends of many years: Fr. Adrian Van Kaam, C.S.Sp., founder of the Institute of Formative Spirituality at Duquesne University; and Dr. Susan Muto, who, together with Fr. Van Kaam, founded the Epiphany Association in Pittsburgh. Dr. Muto's work, *Blessings That Make Us Be* (Crossroad, St. Bede), provided much of the inspiration for these conferences and I strongly recommend it to anyone interested in the

Beatitudes. At this very time Fr. Van Kaam and Dr. Muto are completing a new and powerful work, *Divine Guidance* (Servant), which presents the Beatitudes as directives that indicate the different conditions necessary for following the guidance of God. This new work focuses more on the spiritually formative aspect of the Beatitudes, while my book is centered on the moral challenges arising from the divinely-given directives.

I am also very grateful to the Carmelite nuns of Elysburg, Pennsylvania, and especially to Sister Angela Pikus, O.C.D., and Sister Josephine Koeppel, O.C.D., for providing much information on Blessed Edith Stein. Thanks also goes to Sister Boniface Adams, S.S.F., for much information on the life and cause of Mother Henriette Delille and to Mother Eugenia, F.H.M., for personal memoirs of Mother Theodore Williams. I am grateful to Sister Catherine Walsh, S.C., and John Lynch of St. Joseph's Seminary, Dunwoodie, for research on sources. I am also very grateful to Catherine Murphy of Trinity Retreat for much typing.

The Beatitudes are about justice and righteousness, about peace and forgiveness, about mourning and hunger and thirst. During the past thirty years as a priest, I have met very sincere people who were willing to step out of their comfortable lives for the cause of civil rights, for peace and justice, for morality and human dignity, for faith and truth, for life and mercy. From letter writing campaigns to picket lines, I have met people of many religious affiliations who felt called to take a stand out of a sense of justice and right for others. These causes ranged from the rights of God to the rights of unborn babies. I am grateful to all these people who cared. They were the Holy Spirit's instruments for teaching me about the Beatitudes, preached by Our Lord Jesus Christ in Galilee so long ago and still echoing down the ages.

Fr. Benedict J. Groeschel, C.F.R.
St. Crispin Friary
Bronx, New York
June 24, 1994, Feast of St. John the Baptist

*Blessed are the poor in spirit, for theirs is the kingdom of heaven.*

*Blessed are those who mourn, for they shall be comforted.*

*Blessed are the meek, for they shall inherit the earth.*

*Blessed are those who hunger and thirst for righteousness, for they shall be satisfied.*

*Blessed are the merciful, for they shall obtain mercy.*

*Blessed are the pure in heart, for they shall see God.*

*Blessed are the peacemakers, for they shall be called sons of God.*

*Blessed are those who are persecuted for righteousness' sake, for theirs is the kingdom of heaven.*

**Matthew 5:3-10**

# CHAPTER 1

# *The Way of the Blessed*

*T*his book is about blessedness. It's about a kind of life in which one lives at peace with self, with others, with God. Since very few people attain to a blessed state in their lifetime, this book is also about the long road to blessedness. I will try to explore this subject by offering insights drawn from my reading of the saints and mystics, as well as from my experience as a spiritual director and pastor.

Before we try to sort out what true blessedness is, we must identify what it is *not*. All of us cherish illusions about what will make us happy. Perhaps we fantasize about the exciting and bountiful life of the rich and famous, or the glorious conquests of the powerful. But we must renounce the pursuit of a false blessedness based on such blessings that pass or fade. A little imagination can help here. Let's try to picture what a life of fame, wealth, or power might really be like.

For example, how would it feel to compete in the Winter Olympics as a downhill skier? Since I'm not an athlete, the very thought seems ridiculous: by no stretch of the imagination can I picture my physique as graceful or nimble as an Olympic skier's. Yet I can try to imagine enjoying the magical fame and fortune of the gold medalist.

Can you imagine this kind of happiness or blessedness? Even if you took skiing lessons in your youth, isn't it hard to see yourself actually participating in the Winter Olympics? Picture yourself spending day after day in grueling practice, then soothing your aching body and rising above the sheer exhaustion of such a strenuous schedule. Seriously consider the challenge of having to maintain the self-discipline necessary to keep your body in superb condition—especially when an Italian cheesecake passes right under your nose.

Or what would it be like to be a professional baseball player? I admit that this is not one of my particular fantasies either. When I pass by Yankee Stadium on my way to our friary in the South Bronx, I never give any thought to what it would be like to have seventy thousand people waiting to see me hit the ball. They would have to wait a very long time! Sports fans across the nation, however, may not share my inability to imagine the rigors and rewards of a gifted baseball player's life: the daily practice and discipline, a fat salary, and the adulation of the appreciative crowd.

Yet fame is not an unmixed blessing; it has a dark side. Receiving constant praise and attention can easily distort a person's judgment and self-appraisal. Living under a glaring spotlight quickly becomes tiresome. The lure of sex and drugs is strong, and giving in can lead to disastrous consequences. Fame can end as suddenly as it began, or even turn to infamy if the current idol is caught in a shameful act.

## BLESSINGS THAT PASS

Fame is one kind of blessing that passes. Two others are wealth and power. Indeed, some people enjoy all three at once. Taking a closer look at these fragile blessings might shatter some common illusions about what brings happiness in this life.

**Rags to riches.** Although I've never pictured myself as an athlete, I have occasionally imagined what it might be like to possess great wealth, one of the supreme values of American culture. The actress Mae West—who is rarely quoted in spiritual books (in fact, this may be the *only* time)—used to say, "I've been poor and I've been rich. Rich is better." (I'm told that Mae died after receiving the sacraments of the Catholic Church, having lived her final years with sorrow.)

Deeply embedded in our capitalistic mentality lies the notion that God rewards the righteous with worldly riches. This belief has even infected the Church. Certain evangelists entice their audiences with an unadorned "prosperity gospel." One preacher I read about tosses baskets of dollar bills into his audience of simple souls to emphasize his belief that material wealth is part of our spiritual heritage. Adherents of many non-Christian religions also regard wealth as a sign of divine favor.

Even without knowing anyone extremely wealthy, most of us have enjoyed some small taste of such a life. For instance, computerized overbooking may assign you to a seat in the first-class section of a wide-body jet. While the poor sardines are packed twelve abreast in the back, you comfortably recline and await your complimentary glass of champagne. While they grumble at the dull cuisine of the skies, you savor your succulent filet mignon. While they rub elbows and squirm to relax, you peacefully nod off to sleep. So who ever claimed that life was fair?

My grandmother, a lady of modest means but lots of spirit, used to drag her grandchildren to expensive department stores in New York City where the clerks treated all customers as if they were wealthy. She loved the attention. One of my friends worked as a sales clerk in an expensive shop. He had been coached on how to cater to people—wealthy or not—who wanted to buy something for three times more than they would have spent on it only a few blocks away. The trick was to make the customer feel completely satisfied with such extravagance, and actually pity the poor peons down the street who had to settle for second-rate merchandise and shoddy service.

Entertaining guests by hiring a caterer provides another eye-opener into the world of the wealthy. A professionally attired waiter or waitress serving all sorts of delicious delicacies will help you pretend for a few hours that you are rich. Then when you have to pay the bill, you quickly taste what it's like to be absolutely broke! Even so, you may consider that brief time of lavish pampering worth every penny. You may even sigh heavily as you dream about how wonderful it must be to enjoy the blessedness of freedom from financial cares.

But don't stop dreaming until you can also imagine the flip side of wealth. Actually, being rich can be quite awful. Many wealthy people have complained to me about the difficult burden of riches. Because they have a lot more to lose, the affluent may fret constantly about their investment portfolios or financial empires. The inevitable hardships of life loom especially large to those who have long been accustomed to comfort. Perhaps the heaviest burden of wealth is being separated from a good deal of life by artificial screens, like chauffeur-driven limousines and armed guards at the front gate.

A man who once arrived at my office in a chauffeur-driven Mercedes-Benz reminded me that money might bring *comfort*, but it never brings *happiness*. Yet if we are poor or even middle-class, we may not have learned this lesson. We are likely to presume that wealth would make us happy. It would not. Affluence would probably burden us in the same way it burdens most of the wealthy—except for those fortunate few who are wise enough to live as if they were *not* wealthy and who spend their time doing good for others. Beware: hungry sharks often lurk in the frothy wake of riches, searching for easy prey.

**Being the boss.** Even easier than fantasizing about the blessedness of wealth is pretending what it would be like to be the boss. Perhaps even more people would like to be in charge than would like to be rich. Then you would get to make the rules! Fantastic? Not necessarily. In recent years I have been privileged to work with many bishops and religious leaders who take their duties very seriously. Charged with important areas of responsibility, they are nonetheless aware of how little control they actually have. Consequently, they suffer enormous frustration.

As a matter of fact, those who have lesser responsibilities may find it easier to maintain an illusion of power. The lady in charge of the hotel cleaning crew can be just as dictatorial as Catherine the Great. It's just that she has fewer subjects who bow to her demands. The theater ticket collector can run the whole operation like the czar of Russia. The janitor can claim kinship with Napoleon. And, at least in New York City, these plentiful functionaries often do!

In our pursuit of power, however, what we seldom stop to consider is the extreme discomfort of being in charge. Most of us, at least subconsciously, resent the person at the top. Some of us are nearly green with envy. Have you ever noticed all the Monday-morning quarterbacks who think they could have done a better job of playing Saturday night's game? Even in the Church—perhaps *especially* in the Church—bishops and religious superiors are targets of endless criticism from those who are convinced they could have handled a messy situation more smoothly.

A man with substantial responsibilities once described the common plight of those in charge. He said to me, "You know, when you start with those who are able and those who are willing, and then subtract those who are *able but unwilling* as well as those who are *willing but unable,* you don't have very many people left."

Believe me, it isn't much fun being where the buck stops. The inherent problems and pain usually far outweigh the perks. Misunderstanding, resentment, petulance, and an insatiable need for recognition—such factors make the task of responsible Christian leadership most unenviable, even if the majority of the group being led are sincere believers.

## THE GREATEST OF THESE IS LOVE

If fame, wealth, and power don't lead inevitably to happiness, what about love? Nothing seems to capture our imaginations like a beautiful love story, especially when true devotion overcomes overwhelming obstacles and delivers someone from terrible bondage.

A wealthy friend once asked me to show him what life was like for the poor. I took him to visit an impoverished family living in the depths of Harlem, a young couple with four small children. On a modest salary they managed to maintain an apartment four flights up in an old tenement building. They had filled the few rooms with bits and pieces of furniture purchased from the St. Vincent de Paul thrift shop or donated through missions like those run by the religious order I belong to. The walls were decorated largely with art projects the children had done in school. Their home was very humble, but the children were loved and the family was happy.

I noticed a long look of sadness on my wealthy friend's face and took it for compassion. "I guess you feel very sorry for these people," I commented as we walked down the stairs together.

"By no means," he immediately replied. That sadness I had seen on his face meant something quite different. Although my friend had been blessed with an excellent education, a fine career, and financial security, he told me he had never seen nor experienced the kind of love communicated by that little family, who possessed so few of this world's goods. His sad expression had reflected not compassion for *them* but pity for *himself.*

Unlike riches or power, being truly loved by even one person brings a real happiness. Some have found it, and others can only try to imagine the exquisite joy of being cherished without reservation. Even so, no one experiences love in its fullness. And, as everyone knows who has lost a loved one to death, even this great happiness can be taken away.

I was asked to perform the funeral service of a black woman who had lived to a ripe old age. I had known her family in Harlem for years. I met her elderly husband outside the funeral parlor as he came hobbling along. When we approached the casket together, he stopped and looked lovingly at the body of his dear wife. He began to weep in the most dignified way and said quietly, "She was the best woman in the whole world, the very best."

This was a truly loving couple. They had neither success nor wealth nor power, but they had shared a bountiful love. Yet this man's happiness had come to an end, at least in this life. Fortunately, he looked forward in faith to another happiness, to a blessedness that no one could take away from him. It is that imperishable blessedness that we will be pondering in the pages of this book.

## THE LIMITS OF BEING LOVED

It is worth mentioning at this point that we sometimes equate love with public acclaim, perhaps for a political figure or a media star. Sometimes we heap adulation on a follower of Jesus, the only person ever to walk this earth who loved everyone perfectly.

Mother Teresa, a model of utmost humility, has received unprecedented praise for her simple yet profound words and her countless works of mercy on behalf of the poor. The whole world seemed to love Pope John XXIII, a humble disciple of Jesus who tried to be a spiritual father figure to all. St. Francis served Christ in a spirit of meekness and self-sacrifice but was paradoxically the most popular religious figure of his time.

On the other hand, only a few of the saints enjoyed the happiness of being loved and accepted. Most routinely endured the ugliest taunts and deepest torments. They experienced the deep suffering of social outcasts: rejected by their closest associates, by their own families, by fellow members of their religious communities—perhaps even the communities they had founded.

In any case, outward adulation and love are not accurate indicators of a person's interior journey. The autobiography of the much-beloved Pope John XXIII reveals a man who struggled with a deep sense of worthlessness, often amplified by his keen personal sensitivity. Expecting the story of a happy man in his *Journal of a Soul*,[1] readers were startled to discover a life of constant repentance and self-confrontation, lightened only by the most profound trust in the mercy of God and the grace of Christ. Reading Pope John's autobiography could dispel any illusions entertained by those who mistake a light-hearted exterior for a life without struggle.

We can imagine ourselves in these scenarios of happiness: from wealth, power, and acclaim, which are so glittering but ultimately empty, to tender love, which is so precious but passing. Do any of these earthly blessings resonate with the desires of your own heart? What do *you* most long for in this life? What would make you truly happy? For me, the most desirable, the most meaningful of all these kinds of blessedness is to love and be loved.

As we have seen, however, even the blessedness of human love is transitory. We must search somewhere else if we would find the peace and fulfillment, the happiness that never fails or passes away. Let's examine the only source of such happiness.

## TRUE AND LASTING HAPPINESS: BLESSEDNESS

Jesus, in the Sermon on the Mount, gives us the secret of happiness or blessedness in the Beatitudes. "How happy are the poor in spirit," read some translations of Jesus' words. I find that this translation fails to capture the essence of the message. "Happy" is defined in *Webster's Seventh Dictionary* as "favored by luck or fortune." Now, being loved or rich or powerful may be partly a matter of good luck, but you could never build the kingdom of God on such a flimsy foundation.

The Beatitudes speak of something far greater than happiness: that mysterious reality called *blessedness*. But what does this enigmatic word mean? *Webster's* defines it as "enjoying the bliss of heaven." Some people don't find it hard to imagine this type of happiness. They say to me, "Well, you know, I have experienced blessedness. I have at odd moments been truly happy, blessed, even joyful in my poverty before God." Or they may say, "I have experienced God's peace in the midst of mourning the loss of a loved one." I myself have known such moments of blessedness. If you have as well, then you may have had a true taste of the bliss of heaven.

On the other hand, you may have been struggling with the spiritual life for years or decades. Even after taking the Beatitudes very seriously, you may wonder what Our Lord means when he says "blessed." Because of the ongoing pain of your everyday struggles, you may strain to imagine what such a life would be like—while perhaps outwardly going through the motions, desperately trying to live as a Christian.

Which of these descriptions best characterizes you? Have you been blessed a little bit, or are you still wondering what the Christian life really means? I suspect most of us fall somewhere in the middle. Whatever your personal experience, the pages that follow will help you focus on the answers we find in the Scriptures, especially in the words and teachings of Jesus Christ.

What would it mean to actually find and live the happiness of being poor in spirit, of obtaining mercy, of trying to live as a child of God? The Beatitudes hold out a foretaste of God's goodness for the taking, a way of holding onto a bit of heaven in our hands. Even if you're not able to imagine a life of fame or wealth or power or genuine love, I hope you will be able to imagine what it is like to be one of the blessed.

Dr. William Barclay, the Protestant scholar who has written many helpful biblical commentaries, takes up the question of what it means to be blessed, or happy.[2] Barclay points out that "blessed" in Greek is the word *makarios* and that this word literally means "how filled with bliss." The Greeks called their gods "makarios"—the blessed ones who lived in imaginary places of total happiness named the "blessed isles."

St. Paul calls God "makarios," the blissful one (1 Tm 6:15). Barclay describes this blessedness, then, as the complete bliss of those who have the life of God dwelling within them. They are those who know the presence of Christ working through them as the peacemaker and breaking through as the one who patiently suffers persecution. As they have surrendered to Christ's call, his merciful love has broken open their hearts to transform them, bringing a bliss which the world cannot give. Can you and I aspire to that blessedness, and even in the course of time approach it more closely?


## HELP FOR THE ROUGH ROAD TO HOLINESS

Even if I can't picture myself as an alpine skier, a priest *is* supposed to know what it's like to live as a true Christian... right? To tell the truth, I'm just as awkward as the next person when it comes to knowing how to dwell authentically in the Spirit of God. Perhaps this is precisely because such a life is not just an occasional performance but an unending challenge. Jesus calls us to love perfectly day in and day out, in good times and in bad. You think being a skier or even a world leader is hard! I firmly believe that living as a true Christian is the toughest vocation of all.

We Americans often pretend to know a lot more about certain things than we really do. From time to time and for their own purposes, politicians or policymakers try to convince us that we do in fact live in a Judeo-Christian society, one based on the Bible. Far from it. We seldom hear much about what it really means to live a Christian life. And so churchgoers, who may *look* so much better than "practicing sinners," sometimes leap to a gigantic but faulty presumption of their own righteousness.

We can be "true Christians" in the sense of having received Christ as Savior, yet have miles to walk before becoming truly holy. God accepts us as righteous in Christ, but our outward actions fall far short of his glory. "None is righteous, no, not one," Scripture tells us (Rom 3:10). We need to be transformed in our minds and hearts—a task that requires a lifetime.

Few of us, I'm sure, would be so bold as to claim to be "perfect Christians" in the sense of absolute holiness. Most of us struggle toward this good throughout our lives without ever feeling we have arrived. And that is just as it should be. Holiness shimmers like an illusive oasis before parched wanderers in the desert, until we come at last before the heavenly throne of God and drink deeply from the life-giving water flowing from Jesus Christ.

But every once in a while, we hear of someone who comes close to the ideal—perhaps someone like Mother Teresa, who patiently toils among the poor of the world. Then we might stop to wonder, *what does it feel like to truly live as a Christian?*

Is there any way to know? Or will the life of faith forever remain an enigma? While on some level the Christian life will always be a profound mystery to every believer, God doesn't leave us wandering around in the dark. He is a loving Father who wants to shine light on our paths so that we can come home to live with him forever.

Like an onion, the mystery of what it's like to truly live as a Christian contains deeper and deeper layers of questions wrapped up inside. How do I *become* a true Christian? How do I become a *better* Christian? How do I let the mind of Christ be formed within me? How do I come to know real blessedness?

The answers can be found in the Beatitudes, a few nuggets of wisdom that go light-years beyond the self-help guides that fill the bookshelves of so many struggling people. Sacred Scripture differs dramatically from any other kind of advice or counsel: the teachings of Christ hold power to light a fire inside each one of us. At the end of our lives, these nuggets of truth will carry the power to deliver us from death—because they are not the words of mere men and women, nor even of saints. The words we read in Scripture are the words of God.

Dr. Susan Muto, a founding professor at the Institute of Formative Spirituality in Duquesne, has written a remarkable book entitled *Blessings That Make Us Be: Studies of the Beatitudes*. She describes the Beatitudes as "the invitation from a personal God to each one of us as persons calling us to the destiny of peace and joy."[3] Fr. Adrian Van Kaam of the same institute has described them as having a "formative power." I am deeply indebted to Fr. Van Kaam and Dr. Muto for their very creative insights into the formative power of the Beatitudes.

The Beatitudes, they point out, do not give specifics about the *way* to do something—such as how to ski, how to keep the house beautiful, how to be happy in difficult circumstances, or how to lose weight. They indicate the way, and they carry within them the *power* to form and transform us. In some mysterious way, the Beatitudes not only *tell* us the way, they *pull* us along the way. Like an airport conveyor belt, they pick us up and carry us along with the power of the Spirit. Like an unseen force, they draw us closer to God, like a magnetic field draws metal.

No one can ponder or experience the Beatitudes in this way without bending his or her neck to believe in the power of God. Once this happens, faith fills the believer's being and the person becomes capable of a radical transformation.

The Beatitudes are symbolic pointers, at the same time transforming us deeply and directing us toward the kingdom of God within us. Without this power, a person's attempt to be a good Christian is a sad and sorry thing. We have all seen it... and perhaps even experienced it ourselves. Have you ever met a sincere person who, through misguided effort, ended up like a "plastic Jesus" figurine on a dashboard—molded to external perfection but hollow inside? Unfortunately, endless energy can be expended without much result, like wasted water flowing right down an unstoppered drain.

Truly living as a Christian is not some sort of righteousness that we slip on like an overcoat, nor some ideal we arrive at by means of our own efforts. The life of Christ is a vibrant, powerful, inner force that bubbles up out of the very depths of our being and enables us to do otherwise impossible things, blessed things.

This divine grace gradually helps us to overcome sin, temptations, weaknesses—difficulties and deficits against which we may have struggled all of our lives. Because of this divine power that operates on the human heart with the precision of a surgeon's knife, we are able to rise above our human limitations and receive a glimpse of our heavenly inheritance.

## THE GREAT STONE FACE

Does all this seem a bit abstract? Let me describe the transforming power of Christ by telling a story by New England writer Nathaniel Hawthorne. Hawthorne's writings often reveal his strong Calvinist upbringing, but he has an unexpected link with Catholics through his daughter, a convert and a woman of impressive spiritual stature: Mother Rose Hawthorne Lathrop, who founded the Dominican Sisters, Servants for the Relief of Incurable Cancer.[4]

Hawthorne wrote a story about a young boy named Ernest who grew up in a little village nestled beneath a cliff by the sea.[5] When the setting sun cast its deepening shadows on this particular cliff, the rock bore the likeness of a human face marked with peaceful, gentle, mysteriously exquisite features. The local people passed down the legend that someday the man whose face appeared in the cliffs would actually visit their village.

Ernest studied this face all his life, patiently waiting for the fulfillment of the legend. He would go down to the sea when the trading ships came in, looking for that peaceful face. He died at an old age, very disappointed because the man seen in the cliff had never arrived.

But when Ernest was laid out in his casket, everyone stared at him in amazement and proclaimed, "That's the face in the cliff!" Having pondered this face all his life, Ernest had gradually been formed and fashioned by it. His desires had changed him; he had become what he was looking for.

The Beatitudes carry that same power. Do you long for the blessings they promise? Being comforted and satisfied. Receiving mercy. Becoming children of God. Inheriting the kingdom of heaven. Seeing God. Because the Beatitudes are the Word of God, earnestly watch for them in your life and they will slowly change you. You will be like Ernest.

If Hawthorne could have seen such a face in this world, it might have resembled the face I saw on a statue in front of the state capitol in Hawaii. The face is marked, disfigured, swollen, twisted, and eaten away with leprosy—but it is a strikingly glorious face bearing the marks of divine favor. It is the face of Fr. Damien of Molokai, a selfless missionary who left his native land for the islands of the South Pacific, to search for Jesus crucified and risen. He looked not in the palaces of the wealthy nor the offices of the powerful, but among the poorest and most suffering outcasts of humanity.

Fr. Damien served the lepers of Hawaii. He literally condemned himself to spend the rest of his natural days on an island leper colony which the law prevented him from leaving. He finally contracted leprosy and died among the people he had loved and served so humbly.[6]

On my way to the Far East for a conference several years ago, I stopped in Honolulu and saw Fr. Damien's statue, as well as the cathedral where he was ordained a priest. Later in the day, as our plane took off from Honolulu, the pilot announced, "Ladies and gentlemen, if you look out to the right you will see the island of Molokai and a strip of beach, home of the leper colony where Fr. Damien did his work."

Peeking through the clouds we could see a very high, dark cliff and a little beach. From that distance it looked like paradise. Indeed, through the loving labors of Fr. Damien, aided by the Franciscan sisters and other volunteers, Molokai had been transformed into something of a paradise for those afflicted by a miserable disease.

I was thinking about Fr. Damien all during the flight to Western Samoa, where I was to give my first retreat at Apia. When I arrived at this port town on a beautiful Pacific island, I was utterly astonished to discover that another one of my heroes had died there: Robert Louis Stevenson, who wrote *Kidnapped* and *The Black Arrow*, stories that thrilled me as a boy. Stevenson is buried at Apia next to the cloistered Carmelite convent at the top of a hill. When he died, hundreds of Samoans cut a path through the dense jungle so that this revered man could be buried there. Cut in a single night, the path is called "The Way of the Loving Heart."

I reflected on the mysterious parallels between the lives of Stevenson, a Presbyterian from Scotland, and Fr. Damien, a Catholic from Belgium. Both men died on remote islands surrounded by the native people they had loved. Both were deeply venerated by those they had served.

Then I remembered that their lives had once touched in an unusual way. It happened when a Honolulu clergyman circulated the rumor that Fr. Damien had been unchaste. The story had absolutely no foundation.

The irony of such an accusation of hidden sin is that Fr. Damien is the only person I know of who routinely made public confessions. Since Molokai was completely cut off, Fr. Damien would take his little boat out to meet a steamer where his confessor stood on the deck. Forbidden to come aboard because of spreading contagion, Fr. Damien had to shout out his confessions for the world to hear. Fr. Damien's life was an open book.

Upon hearing the false accusation, Stevenson—who had never met Fr. Damien but knew his work—rushed to the priest's defense. He wrote a public letter denouncing the clergyman who had started the rumor. (In an absolute masterpiece of irony, Stevenson's letter was presented as an example of supreme invective when I studied English literature.)

How blessed was this saintly priest! I saw a photograph of him stretched out in bed on the day of his death. (By that time the Franciscan sisters had come to nurse him, along with a few other priests and his faithful helper Ira Dutton, also known as "Brother Joseph.") Fr. Damien's face is eaten away and twisted, his body misshapen, his arms no longer useful at all. But his face bears a look of peace, gentleness, bliss—just like the great stone face on the lava cliff.

By the grace of God, the neglected lepers that Fr. Damien served helped to form him into what he had so desired—the face of Christ. This man, so merciful and so persecuted, learned meekness in spite of his own great temper. By the grace of God he brought peace to an island that was a living hell. As I write these lines the people of Hawaii and of Belgium are rejoicing that Fr. Damien is about to be beatified, honored for his work among the suffering of Molokai.

As Dr. Barclay renders the Beatitudes, "O the bliss of the merciful, for they shall obtain mercy. O the bliss of the peacemakers, for they shall be called the children of God. O the bliss of those who suffer persecution for justice's sake, for they shall be filled."[7]

Can you honestly imagine being formed by the Beatitudes, as Fr. Damien and others were formed by them? The promise is glorious, but the price is steep. May the Holy Spirit guide your study of the Beatitudes so that you may know more of that divine bliss. May we who know that bliss in only the vaguest way become more and more filled with blessedness as the form of Jesus Christ takes shape in our own souls. When others see us, may they see the face of Jesus Christ etched in human flesh.

*Holy Spirit, you are with me since my Baptism. Yet how seldom do I raise my mind to your presence. Nonetheless, you are within me, forming and enlightening me in all the events of life when I freely let you do so. But you will not force yourself upon me; you lead me by a light and not by a chain. You call to my heart by the words of the Messiah, Our Lord Jesus Christ. You strengthen me and form me by these mysterious words which shape me as the words of the Creator shaped the waste and void into the living earth. O Holy and Mysterious Spirit, I am so weak and so blind, so poor and so much in conflict with myself. Breathe on me, O Spirit, and I shall be renewed. Touch me with your grace and I shall be made whole again. Enlighten me and I shall see all that blinds me. Lift me and I shall run in the way of your commandments. Amen.*

# CHAPTER 2

# *Written on Our Hearts*

W hat matters most when you're looking to buy a new house? Any real estate agent will tell you: location, location, location. We can say the same of Scripture. We cannot examine the Beatitudes apart from their relationship to the whole Word of God. We can't just pull these verses out of context. Let's examine some vital issues about these precious nuggets of gold which promise to put a bit of heaven in our hands.

First of all, the Gospel of St. Matthew places the Beatitudes at the beginning of the section called "the Sermon on the Mount" (Mt 5-7). When I was a seminarian, I was disappointed to learn that Jesus probably never preached such a sermon, or, if he did, that it was much shorter than the one in Matthew.

According to most orthodox Scripture scholars, these verses appear to be a collection of the moral teachings of Christ, arranged in what is called a *didache* (pronounced did-a-kay), from the same root as "didactic." (There is, in fact, a book called *The Didache*, a summary of the moral teaching of the early Church.) These particular instructions in the New

Testament were apparently put together some years after Our Lord had risen from the dead, and then grouped around the account of the Sermon on the Mount.

In St. Luke's Gospel, these same teachings are contained in the sermon on the *plain*. They are very similar except that the eight sayings are rendered as four Beatitudes and four warnings: "Woe to you that are rich.... Woe to you who laugh now..." (Lk 6:17-26).

Perhaps you grew up thinking that all of Christ's statements in the Bible were taken down in shorthand by a secretary or transcribed on a machine like in a courtroom trial. Or perhaps they were captured on tape by some disciple who miraculously possessed some precursor of a cassette recorder! Comparing one Gospel to another reveals that these are false assumptions. Often, as with the Beatitudes, the same teachings are rendered in different forms.

Scholars have concluded that in some instances Scripture does record the exact words of Christ. They call these the *ipsissima verba*, the very words. But the Sermon on the Mount is not a word-for-word transcription. It is a summary of Our Lord's moral teaching. It is his very *voice* rather than his very words. And this is true even though the original setting when he spoke was different from the one described by the evangelist.

Fr. John Meier, a well-known Scripture scholar, explains this theory in his book, *The Vision of Matthew*.[1] According to Fr. Meier, there is a crucial link between the Beatitudes and Jesus' claims of ultimate authority. Christ's opening words in the Sermon on the Mount show him to be the herald of the kingdom of God. Through this collection of moral teachings, Jesus consistently proclaims himself to be the person who gives the law in the place of God.[2]

Through the Beatitudes, Christ promises true happiness to his disciples. But has the perfectly happy individual described ever existed in fact? Just once, says Fr. Meier. The only perfect person was the one who uttered the Beatitudes: Christ himself is the blessed man.[3]

## ARE THESE BLESSINGS REALLY ATTAINABLE?

If the Beatitudes are so difficult that only Christ himself has fulfilled them, then why did he lay out such promises? Aren't they actually devoid of meaning if none of us can really expect to be perfectly poor in spirit or perfectly forgiving or perfectly adept at making peace?

Take time right now to read through the whole Sermon on the Mount. I guarantee that you'll be depressed. You'll say, "I couldn't ever, even if I lived a thousand years, possibly live up to this sermon."

Some Protestant writers, observes renowned Lutheran scholar Joachim Jeremias, have suggested that the Sermon on the Mount is so utterly unattainable precisely to convince us that it is impossible for us to be saved. In other words, Christ put these burdens on us and then said in effect, "Well, you can't do it. But now you know what it's like to be saved." It seems to me that such an interpretation falls short of the "good news" of salvation!

Doctor Jeremias points out that the good news of the gospel includes not only the moral teaching of Christ but also the proclamation that he is the Savior. This is a very crucial point, one which easily flies over our heads.[4]

If Christ only preached the doctrine in the Sermon on the Mount without ever proclaiming himself the Savior of the world, says Dr. Jeremias, then we would indeed bear an impossible burden. But the gospel assures us that we cannot save ourselves. Even with the help of Christ, we are not our own saviors. *Christ alone is the Savior of the world.* He promises that his grace will well up inside us, that he can and will transform us and make us into what we are not.

Just think of the incredible blessings contained in the Beatitudes: to see God, to be called a child of God. And we are promised this glorious destiny not by a priest at Baptism, nor reassured by a bishop at Confirmation; God himself makes the promise through the sacred Scriptures. Aren't these the blessings you truly long for?

Clearly, Christianity is not just another nice religion, not just one of a number of ways to God. The Sermon on the Mount, and especially the Beatitudes, makes this quite plain. The challenge they issue becomes comprehensible only if we take into account the last things: death and what lies beyond. As the flame of natural life flickers out, it is replaced by the dawn of eternal life. Ultimately, you and I will taste that bliss, that happiness, that joy promised in the Beatitudes—only on the other side of this vale of tears.

Only in the hereafter will heaven truly be in our hands. Meanwhile, we have to work for it here on this earth. Fr. Meier sums up this challenge very well:

> Matthew's Gospel continually presents the church and the individual Christian with a salutary shock. The radical demands of Christ in his gospel summoned both the institutional and individual believers out of the reasonable lifestyles of this world including the world's great religions.
>
> The uncompromising radicalism of Christ's moral message in Matthew is a challenge to all of us to realize in our own lives that the word eschatological is more than theological jargon. [The word "eschatological" means that which is true on the other side, after the *eschaton*, that is after the end of all earthly things.] It is the designation for the total change the Son of Man brings any time he comes into his church and into the lives of individual believers.[5]

There is no namby-pamby pablum, easily digested by mere babes in the faith. This is precisely why we don't often hear the

Beatitudes preached these days.

One evening some friends and I stopped outside a cafe with a sign in the window that advertised "cappuccino"—a strong Italian coffee laced with cream. Since this delectable beverage is named after the Capuchin friars, I happen to be partial to it. (For many years I myself wore the brown robe after which this delicious coffee is named.) At my urging, we entered the cafe—without knowing that we had to walk through a bar to get to where they served the cappuccino.

Several people at the bar seemed understandably startled when I came through looking like an advertisement for the *Canterbury Tales*. But one fellow who was a little bit tipsy looked up and said, "Hey, Padre, wait a minute. We're having an argument here. Don't you think that Matthew was a pain in the neck?"

That was the last question I ever expected to hear in a bar! I was taken aback and had to answer that I had never really thought about Matthew that way. But once I had given the man's question some thought, I realized that Christ's words *are* tough indeed! Christ puts forth a thoroughly demanding and radical message in Matthew's Gospel. Yet on the other side of that toughness lies the *promise*. To paraphrase it somewhat: "How blessed are the poor in spirit; they will get into the kingdom of heaven. How blessed are those who suffer persecution; they will get into the kingdom too." That is the promise. If you ever want to make serious headway in the spiritual life, you will have to take the Beatitudes—both the challenge and the promise—very much to heart.

## SIGNPOSTS ALONG THE WAY

According to Dr. Susan Muto, the Beatitudes relate to the three traditional phases of the spiritual life, sometimes known as the "three ways." The *purgative* stage is the initial phase, through which most people are struggling. The middle or *illuminative* stage marks a decisive turning point when the power of God comes down upon a Christian with great power. The third way is called the *unitive* stage, when a believer mysteriously walks as a saint—as much as is possible here on this earth. (For a more detailed explanation, see my book, *Spiritual Passages*.)

This very ancient teaching about the spiritual life goes back at least to the early Fathers of the Church such as St. Gregory of Nyssa and St. Augustine. Many see it reflected in the writings of St. Paul as well. Serious seekers of God will find this teaching of the three ways to be very helpful in their own spiritual growth.

**The first way: putting the axe to the root of sin.** Briefly, the first way is marked by various phases of purification, or "purgation." Once a person has been awakened to grace by a new life—or at least to a new freshness of fervor or commitment—he or she enters into a process of being purified from all deliberate sin, even from sin caused by human weakness—"sins unto death" and "sins unto sorrow," I call them.

Although this process is never entirely completed in this lifetime, the person's will gradually turns more and more from self to God, motivated and strengthened by grace. Over time, the believer's faith matures into a serene and grateful acceptance of all the revealed mysteries; there is no longer the need either to rationalize them or to set them in the mind so clearly that the true light of faith is artificially limited by human concepts.

Finally, at the last step of the first way comes the great struggle to truly trust God, to believe and hope that in all of life's events and circumstances, he will bring us and those dear to us to salvation. Be certain that this daunting journey of the first way cannot be accomplished without struggle and the painful defeat of our own egotism. Even a little growth is rarely gained without suffering. But for most seekers of God, the pains and sufferings of life become powerful forces that prod them along

Most sincere believers are somewhere in this process of purification. If we are impressed by their selflessness, they are probably nearer the end of this phase of their spiritual journey. Yet the search for true blessedness has only begun.

**The second way: light at the end of the tunnel.** During the second or illuminative way, the believer who has become open to Christ's presence experiences God's light penetrating the soul. Although far from being a saint, he or she more obviously radiates the light of Christ to a darkened world. The person's works of charity and forgiveness grow more numerous.

Gradually, toward the end of the second way, a profound, gripping, even compelling spirit of quiet prayer dominates this grace-filled life. Observers begin to consider the person saintly—yet time and again they feel disappointed because of the inconsistencies, weaknesses, and even sins they cannot help but notice. All saints have passed through this phase to some degree—as their families, friends, or close companions could testify!

At the end of the second way, the individual has given up to God all the aspects of self that are under conscious control. He or she surrenders joyfully and without hesitation in order to possess the Holy Trinity, whose presence is so powerfully experienced in interior prayer. Then, just when all seems sweetness and light, this beautiful way crashes down into the darkness of the apparent absence of grace. The last days of that remarkable spiritual prodigy, St. Thérèse of Lisieux, seem to reflect this inexplicable descent into darkness.

**The third way: becoming united to God.** This poor soul is then led by the powerful virtues of faith and hope and sustained by love of God. Without any trace of self-fulfillment, the believer trudges on in darkness and gradually becomes united to God in the third way, the unitive stage. Even if someone were at only the beginning of this way, calling that man or woman a saint would not be far from reality. Such a believer has purchased the pearl of great price, has found in the darkness the *presence* of God instead of merely the *image* of his presence.

I believe that only a few extraordinarily blessed souls enter the upper stages of this union with God in their lifetimes. We dimly perceive this greatness in larger-than-life figures such as Paul, Ignatius of Antioch, Augustine, Francis, Clare, the two Catherines (of Siena and of Genoa), Teresa, and John of the Cross.

Usually unnoticed by the vast majority of human beings, this spiritual journey is in fact the most profound of human accomplishments. Here and there in life you may meet some person—most often utterly unknown to the world—who has walked this way and gone much further than most sincere Christians. Cardinal John Henry Newman, who may indeed have become a saint himself, recognized this hidden quality of the blessed and their interior journey and described it well:

True Christians look just the same to the world as... the great mass of what are called respectable men... who in their hearts are very different; they make no great show, they go on in the same quiet ordinary way as the others, but really they are training to be saints in heaven. They do all they can to change themselves, to become like God, to obey God, to discipline themselves, to renounce the world; but they do it in secret, both because God tells them so to do, and because they do not like it to be known. Moreover, there are a number of others between these two with more or less of worldliness and more or less of faith. Yet they all look about the same to common eyes, because true religion is a hidden life in the heart; and though it cannot exist without deeds, yet these are for the most part secret deeds, secret charities, secret prayers, secret self-denials, secret struggles, secret victories....

And yet, though we have no right to judge others, but must leave this to God, it is very certain that a really holy man, a true saint, though he looks like other men, still has a sort of secret power in him to attract others to him who are like-minded, and to influence all who have any thing in them like him. And thus it often becomes a test, whether we are like-minded with the Saints of God, whether they have influence over us. And though we have seldom means of knowing at the time who are God's own Saints, yet after all is over we have; and then on looking back at what is past, perhaps after they are dead and gone, if we knew them, we may ask ourselves what power they had over us, whether they attracted us, influenced us, humbled us, whether they made our hearts burn within us. Alas! too often we shall find that we were close to them for a long time, had means of knowing them and knew them not, and that is a heavy condemnation on us indeed.... The holier a man is, the less he is understood by men of the world. All who have any spark of living faith will understand him in a measure, and the holier he is, they will, for the most part, be attracted the more; but those who serve the world will be blind to him, or scorn and dislike him, the holier he is.[6]

## POINTERS TO OUR MINDS

The Beatitudes portray a life directed toward saintliness or holiness. They speak to both our minds and our hearts. As pointers to our minds, the eight Beatitudes can be divided into three categories corresponding to the three stages of the spiritual life which I have just described: the purgative, illuminative, and unitive. Rather than looking at the Beatitudes in the order in which they are written, following the lead of Dr. Muto I have chosen to organize this book according to these three categories. As you consider these truths in relationship to your own spiritual life, I hope you come closer to finding the blessings you seek.

Three of the Beatitudes relate to the first way, the purgative stage of cleansing and purification. These tough sayings open the way to a release from sin and finally lead us powerfully out of the purgative way.

> *Blessed are those who mourn, for they shall be comforted.*
> *Blessed are those who hunger and thirst for righteousness,*
> *for they shall be satisfied.*
> *Blessed are those who are persecuted for righteousness' sake,*
> *for theirs is the kingdom of heaven.*

Once we have made some progress in the spiritual life, we will be blessed to cross into the illuminative way. It's kind of like making it to second base. Read on: you may be surprised to discover that this reality seems to be happening in your own life—even though you often feel as if you've never even made it to *first* base! The three bright Beatitudes of the middle way speak to this second stage of being flooded with the light of God.

> *Blessed are the meek, for they shall inherit the earth.*
> *Blessed are the merciful, for they shall obtain mercy.*
> *Blessed are the peacemakers, for they shall be called sons of God.*

The last two Beatitudes direct us into greater holiness, corresponding to the unitive way. These somewhat mystical promises help us to understand the lives of the saints. We begin to perceive how to be more united with God and how to grow in this blessed unity of mind and heart.

> *Blessed are the poor in spirit, for theirs is the kingdom*
> *of heaven.*
> *Blessed are the pure in heart, for they shall see God.*

A paradox emerges as we progress along the road to blessedness. In a sense, the kingdom of heaven becomes tangible; God himself becomes visible. This phenomenon prompted the mystical poet Francis Thompson to exclaim:

O world, intangible, we touch thee,
O world, unknowable, we know thee,
Inapprehensible, we clutch thee! [7]

The Beatitudes are paradoxes in other ways as well. Wherever we find ourselves in this spiritual journey, we cannot help but notice the apparent contradictions bound up in Our Lord's puzzling promises: the poor are rich; those who mourn are blessed; the meek will be powerful; the hungry shall be filled; the persecuted are blessed.

How contrary this is to the messages of the world in which we live. They urge you to pretend to be rich or powerful. They want you to play along when they assure you that you're loved without limit or qualifications when you really are not. For example, the bank offers constant reassurance that you have a friend there, someone who will personally cater to your every need. But try testing how far that relationship will actually go without sufficient collateral to back it up! Multiple roadblocks quickly rise up to hinder your quest for financial help.

The smiling faces on TV seem sincerely solicitous as to whether or not you're able to clean the greasy pots, or polish your kitchen floor to a brilliant shine, or banish all the germs from your bathroom. Don't be fooled. Remember that advertising agencies hire actors and actresses to sell that particular pot scrubber or floor wax or antibacterial cleanser. Oblivious to your personal needs, these players regard you as merely a pawn in the world of marketing, a faceless consumer who holds the money.

Your "friendly neighborhood insurance agents" assure you they have your best interests at heart. Their proffered love and care look so sincere—until you submit a claim and find out what the fine print excludes. You discover that the bottom line may override the best intentions of an insurance agent if the company is to remain in business.

The messages of the Beatitudes are just the opposite of all this make-believe happiness. They are not pretense or empty promises. These few words powerfully open up to us what it really means to live as a Christian, just as the dawning sun pours into an unobstructed window facing east.

## THE BEATITUDES AND THE HOLY SPIRIT

Upon entering the illuminative way in which divine grace floods the heart, the believer will realize that the Beatitudes are inextricably intertwined with the gifts of the Holy Spirit. These seven spiritual gifts, named as qualities of the promised Messiah in Isaiah 11:2-3, are operations of the Holy Spirit. They are mysterious abilities or qualities given to faithful followers of the gospel, graces which enable them to do many things that would be otherwise impossible. These gifts are essential if one is going to lead a faithful Christian life. Indeed, the most profound reality that can come into the life of any person seeking to truly live as a Christian is the gift of the Holy Spirit.

As quoted in John J. Jepson's superb commentary, *The Lord's Sermon on the Mount,* St. Augustine links the operation of specific Beatitudes to particular spiritual gifts.[8] For instance, he says that the poor in spirit have received in abundance the gift of reverence, or fear of the Lord. Those who mourn have received the gift of knowledge, an understanding of what is necessary for us to mourn—and to mourn in a way that will lead to rejoicing.

Have you ever experienced mourning as an occasion for rejoicing? Perhaps you've wept deeply over the loss of someone dear to you. Then right in the middle of your tears, you suddenly understood the truth of salvation in a new way. That was the gift of knowledge, helping you to put these sorrowful events of life into the powerful perspective of eternity.

Augustine considers the first and last Beatitudes as identical, and so he matches the seven gifts and the seven Beatitudes exactly. As we study each Beatitude in order of its place in the spiritual journey, we will also consider the corresponding gift of the Holy Spirit according to St. Augustine. He lists the seven pairs as follows (remember that he considers the first and the last Beatitudes as being the same):

In matching the spiritual gifts with their corresponding Beatitudes, Augustine does not imply that a specific gift is the operational cause of a particular Beatitude. This is the Spirit's

| Gift of the Holy Spirit | | Beatitude |
|---|---|---|
| the fear of the Lord or reverence | 1, 8. | the poor in spirit, and those who are persecuted for righteousness |
| piety or fidelity | 2. | the meek |
| knowledge | 3. | those who mourn |
| fortitude or courage | 4. | those who hunger and thirst for justice |
| counsel | 5. | the merciful |
| understanding | 6. | the pure of heart |
| wisdom | 7. | the peacemakers |

work. He simply notes that an apparent correspondence exists between the two. For example, he writes, "Fortitude corresponds to those who hunger and thirst, for they labor in a desire that comes from what is truly good and in an effort to stem their love for the earthly and corruptible. Hence of them it is said: blessed are they who hunger and thirst after justice."[9]

## THE LAW OF THE SPIRIT OF LIFE

Why this concern about the gifts of the Holy Spirit? The fact is that we cannot successfully continue or even begin to live the life of the Beatitudes unless we are lifted up "on eagles' wings" (Ex 19:4) through the improvement of these spiritual gifts. Many people—including clergy and religious—spend a considerable amount of energy on Christian activities such as prayer and good works, yet don't appear to have a clue as to their ultimate goal, the final destination of their spiritual journey. Even the concept of a spiritual journey often escapes their notice.

Scripture tells us that the gospel abrogated the law given to Moses, and that we follow "the law of the Spirit of life" (Rom 8:2). But if you were to ask most people *where* this law of the Spirit of life is to be found or what it entails, they would be hard pressed to tell you.

Some would guess that the law of the Spirit of life means the Sermon on the Mount, or the whole gospel, or all the teachings included in the sacred tradition of the Church and the apostolic teaching. And in fact, all of these sources represent the external, visible, comprehensible, even printable law, if you will. This visible law guides us and is called the law of Christ. But the Fathers of the Church, in an all-but-forgotten teaching, maintain that the "law of the Spirit of life" is *written on the heart* (or the inner being) of the devout follower of Christ.

St. Paul clearly describes the true location of this law: "you show that you are a letter from Christ delivered by us, written not with ink but with the Spirit of the living God, not on tablets of stone but on tablets of human hearts" (2 Cor 3:3). In Galatians we are told to "walk by the Spirit," and that if we are led by the Spirit, we are "not under the law" (Gal 5:16-18).

St. John Chrysostom in several sermons speaks of the new law as the Holy Spirit himself.[10] St. Augustine wrote an entire treatise, "De Spiritu et Littera," where we find the following summary of this important and little-known doctrine: "What else are the laws of God himself poured into our hearts than the presence itself of the Holy Spirit? By his presence love is poured out into our hearts which is the fullness of the law."[11]

The ultimate location of God's law is *in the heart* (or in the center of being) of the individual believer. This teaching has not been popular because it can be misunderstood easily and lead to moral subjectivism. Yet the Holy Spirit can't write *one* moral law onto my heart and *another* one onto yours. We obviously need the "external" moral teaching of Scripture and tradition to keep us from sinking into a quagmire of confusion. At the same time we must remember that this law is inscribed on our hearts by the Holy Spirit.

## THE FAITH OF THE POOR

As I search my mind for concrete examples of this forgotten teaching, I think of the army of poor, elderly people I have known over the years. These dear souls—mostly women, with little education, and often far removed from contact with the express teaching of the Catholic Church—nevertheless lead lives of great virtue and consistently demonstrate the gifts of the Holy Spirit. They have far surpassed many of us who have studied the law and the prophets and even the Church Fathers and the doctors!

One example will illustrate this point. Mrs. Mac was a kind and generous black lady who lived for over fifty years in the same apartment in Harlem. In her younger days, she and her husband Jimmy would organize baseball leagues for the neighborhood children who had little else to do. Some of the players from the New York Giants helped them by rounding up free tickets and used sports equipment. These professional athletes, heroes in the children's eyes, even showed up occasionally for local events.

In addition to taking wonderful care of her family, Mrs. Mac cared without compensation for several foster children. In many ways, she took a concern for all of the residents in her apartment building. This loving woman seemed to have a healing presence; she made hurting people feel better just by talking to them.

After the long and painful death of her husband, Mrs. Mac decided to refurbish her apartment with a fresh coat of paint and some new furniture. The cost in those days came to about twelve hundred dollars—a sum Mrs. Mac didn't have. But her friend, Rosita, who was a Catholic, suggested that she make a novena, nine days of prayer in honor of the Blessed Mother of Jesus. Even though she was a Protestant, Mrs. Mac agreed.

On the ninth evening, this dear woman dreamed that she looked out her window and saw Jimmy coming down the street. He called up to the fifth floor: "Hey, Maw, the number, the number." Upon awaking, Mrs. Mac recalled that her husband had often placed a two-dollar bet with the local bookie on numbers four, five, and six. Never a gambler herself, Mrs. Mac took the hint nonetheless and sent a youngster around the corner to place her bet. Her winnings that day came to exactly twelve hundred dollars.

After a period of instruction, I received Mrs. Mac into the Catholic Church. This turning point was important but did not change her life in an obvious way. With very little formal teaching, she had followed the law of the Spirit of life in Christ, written in her heart over many years (Rom 8:2).

Where are you in the spiritual journey? Along the first way, perhaps, still struggling with sin and weakness? Does your trust in God's providence sometimes flicker like a flame deprived of oxygen? Are the pain and suffering sometimes more than you think you can bear? Do you ever feel like the candle has gone out altogether, leaving you to stumble along in the dark?

Wherever you may be, keep pressing on. God is bringing you closer to himself. Allow him to bring you life and strength through the Beatitudes. Let him engrave the law of the Spirit of life deeper and deeper into your heart. And remember: *we do not travel alone.*

⁓

*Give me your gifts and lift me up, O Holy Spirit, my Advocate promised to me by Christ himself. I am often cast down, defeated, and broken; often blind and insensitive even to those I love; often caught up foolishly in that which is passing away before my eyes. Spirit of truth, when this road is long and weary and I am fearful and tired, lift me up on your eagle wings so that I may not fail utterly those whom you have given me in this life to influence, to help and to support. Give me your wisdom at every stage of my journey that I may know that you alone make all things new and good and beautiful. Then I shall be a blessing to others and cease to be an obstacle to them and a burden to myself. Amen.*

# CHAPTER 3

# *The First Beatitude of Purification: Cleansing Tears*

*Blessed are they who mourn,*
*for they will be comforted.*

When I was in the fifth grade, I attained what I considered a lofty position: I became an altar boy. Our parish gave each of us a cassock and surplice, which we brought home so that our mothers could sew on buttons and press the linen. I loved to carry these symbolic garments in full view so that people would know that I was an altar boy.

My career as an altar boy reached its pinnacle in eighth grade, when I was appointed to be the cross bearer for the Feast of Corpus Christi. On that day the altar boys wore special robes with buster-brown collars, big bow ties, and white gloves. My home parish had adopted a tradition from a village in Italy of arranging a carpet of rose petals in the shape of a chalice on the sidewalk outside the church. I remember our principal, Mother Dolorita, admonishing me, "Mr. Groeschel, when you walk over those rose petals, do not disturb a single one. Don't move anything."

Unbeknownst to anyone in the congregation—including my own mother—I carried the cross down the sidewalk while walking six inches *above* the rose petals. At least that's how I felt: like I was practically levitating. When I reached the front doors of the church, the chalice design was perfectly undisturbed. Everyone else in the procession walked along the edges. Just the pastor and I—with me leading the way—were privileged to walk right through the rose-petal chalice.

I must admit, that day elevated my self-esteem to dizzying heights. Unfortunately, everything has been downhill since. I naïvely thought that this exceptional day was to be the beginning of a series of great leaps forward. Experience soon disabused me of this notion.

As a seminarian I paid in blood, sweat, and tears for all the fun I had as an altar boy. I endured eight long years of trial and struggle. If anybody was *not* cut out to be a seminarian, it was me. And by the time I was ordained, I knew too much about the responsibilities of the priesthood to ever take the attending adulation very seriously. Besides, all my high school buddies had plenty to say to keep me humble on the day of my first Mass.

## SIFTING THE WHEAT FROM THE CHAFF

If you look back into your own childhood, you are likely to find any number of occasions that contributed to your development. Yet at some point you had to relinquish many of these goods because the intended growth had been accomplished. To hang onto them any longer would have become an obstacle to your personal growth. (I knew one middle-aged woman who still kept her skates just in case she ever decided to go back to the roller derby!)

The first stage of the interior life encompasses the work of purification from this excess baggage in our souls, a work which seems to go on forever. When we are first called by grace and awakened to the reality of God in our lives, we find a tremendous amount of junk and debris in the way. Some of it is just like the old rollerskates: good things that are no longer helpful to our development. Some is not good for us at all.

At whatever age we respond to God's call, the seven capital sins and the pathologies of the soul have exercised a strong pull on us. Faith doesn't suddenly make us immune to the lure of sin. All manner of temptations usually continue to intrude on our behavior despite our best intentions. We constantly come up against the wounds of actual sin and original sin, the sins that we ourselves have committed and the wounds that we received at birth because of being born into a fallen race.

Simply put, every one of us is wounded, sick, and needy whenever God comes to our rescue. Consequently, a great task of purification must take place in our lives. Perhaps the most sensitive and difficult dimension of that task is sorting the good elements from the bad. We all have attachments—things that we love, that we need, that we desire. How in the world do we separate the good from the bad?

An even more difficult question: how do we separate the good affections that are the beginnings of eternity and that will last forever from the good ones that will not last at all? To be perfectly honest, I don't think we can get very far in making these distinctions. No human mind possesses the depth and complexity necessary to determine what should be given up now, what should be held onto for a while longer, and what should be surrendered forever.

I certainly don't know even the next step in my own spiritual life, much less in the life of anyone else. In fact, I don't trust anyone who claims to know the next step in his or her own interior journey. Why? Because the spiritual life is not *our* enterprise. It is the work of *God*. He calls us forward by grace and leads us, one step at a time.

When we first respond to God's call—even if we are young and have always said our prayers—we are filled with a teeming jungle of desires and needs, both noble and ignoble. Among the honorable ones are those that will last forever and those that will pass away. How do we sort them out? The answer is very simple: God will do it. He sifts the wheat from the chaff. The two Beatitudes of purification are often the first tools he uses to sort out the good, the passing, and the bad in our lives.

## SUFFERING AND LOSS

After losing something or someone dear to us, why are we blessed when we mourn? Because God is making room in our lives for eternity. Let me offer the most painful yet realistic example I can imagine.

Consider the rare jewel of a true Christian marriage, one which surpasses any other supportive partnerships. Daily carrying the cross with joy, zeal, perseverance, and mutual sharing, husband and wife walk side by side on their spiritual journey. But no matter how faithful, loyal, and supportive they are to each other, both know that this immense good of human love in Christ must come to an end—at least in terms of this earthly life. In some remote corner of their minds, they are always aware that someday they will have to say goodbye. And they know that the one who is left behind will suffer the greatest pain.

We all know the pain of loss to some degree. You may be a parent who must watch your children grow up and leave home. You may be a teacher who must permit your favorite students to move on to other classes. You may pour yourself out for a cherished project or cause, only to see it die for lack of funding. At some point, all of us must say goodbye to most of the people and things in our lives. Yet our Christian faith assures us that the best part of relationships, of human love, of friendships, of marriage, moves into eternal life. We will find it all in the hands of God... but only after the final purification of death.

Whenever we experience one of these sorrowful losses, painful questions fill our minds. *Could I have done more? Could I have responded differently? Could I have been a better parent? A more loving spouse? More dedicated to my vocation?* The answer is always yes. There is always more good we can do. But when the possibility of doing a particular good comes to an end, our pain over this loss serves a crucial function: mourning activates in our minds a gift of the Holy Spirit, the gift of knowledge. This potent gift enables us to evaluate all of the good things of this world in terms of our eternal goal. This is one reason not to stifle our grief over the serious losses in our lives.

Americans, especially men, consider it something of a disgrace to mourn in public. Parents who are brokenhearted over the loss of a child seldom express their grief to anyone but their closest friends and relatives. A family who is totally dependent on the income from its business is likely to keep its impending collapse a secret. Acquaintances who attend a funeral try to keep a stiff upper lip.

And if people do share their grief, it often prompts condescending remarks. "Oh, poor Charlie broke down at the funeral Mass for his mother." Poor fellow if he didn't break down! Carried to the extreme, the modern denial of suffering and mourning would turn all of our funerals into fiestas. I've been to funerals that actually sickened me because all the festivities and alleluias provided no opportunity for people to sit down and shed real tears of grief. Those who mourned had to go home and weep in secret. How much better if they could have expressed their sorrow to others and received comfort and consolation.

We need to remember the promise of this Beatitude: *blessed* are those who mourn, for they shall be comforted. Mourning is a good and productive activity. It purifies our souls to receive more of God. St. Augustine learned this lesson the hard way.

## TEARS OF MOTHER AND SON

For fifteen years, Augustine indulged in pleasure and pursued worldly knowledge, gradually making his apostasy known to all. He broke his mother's heart in countless ways. He moved into her home with the woman who bore his son. He publicly renounced the Catholic faith and joined a pagan cult. Monica faithfully prayed and fasted for her son's conversion year after year. Seeing him so blatantly reject Christ made her mourn his spiritual death and weep copious tears. But she refused to give up pleading his case before God.

In a dramatic experience of divine grace, Augustine suddenly returned to his faith, was baptized by St. Ambrose, and formally entered the Church. His mother became his dear friend, but soon it was his turn to mourn for her: Monica died in Augustine's thirty-third year. Considering it unseemly to cry at the funeral of one who had died such a holy death, he was plunged into what psychology calls a period of dissociation. Basically, he was so stunned that he couldn't even weep.

Like many Christians of his time, Augustine believed that because of the hope of eternal life, we should not mourn and weep. In time he finally experienced a different reality. He wrote:

Little by little I began to recover my feelings about your handmaid, O Lord. Remembering how loving and devout was her conversation with you, how pleasant and considerate her conversation with me of which I was suddenly deprived, and I found solace in weeping in your sight both about her and for her, about myself and for myself. I no longer tried to check my tears but I let them flow as they would, making a pillow for my heart and it rested upon them, for it was your ear that heard my weeping and not the ears of a man who might have misunderstood my tears and despised them.

O Lord, I confess it to you in writing and let him who reads it interpret it as he will. But if he sees it as a sin that for so small a portion of time I wept for my mother now dead and departed from my sight who had wept for me for so many years that I should live in your sight, let him not scorn me but rather if he is a person of charity, let him weep for my sins to you the Father of all the children of Christ.[1]

St. Augustine was blessed in his mourning. His cleansing tears provided such deep comfort that he described them as a "pillow for his heart." He spoke of true Christian mourning which is filled with a constant remembering of salvation and redemption. Augustine didn't mourn because he had no hope. He mourned because he *did:* because his mother had prayed for thirty years that he would come to know God. He mourned for her and for himself, for all that was still lacking in his spiritual maturity. And he asked most of all that God would continue to cleanse his soul of the obstacles that stood in the way of his attaining the kingdom of heaven.

I believe that most of us do not mourn enough over the loss of our loved ones. Do you remember how seriously Catholics used to pray on All Soul's Day for those who had died? No more. Unfortunately, the notion of the happy hunting ground has infiltrated the contemporary Church, and many Christians believe that we move from this world to the next without any accounting of what we have done with our lives.

In the midst of such spiritual confusion, we lose the ability to truly pray and to mourn for the dead. And when we suffer losses other than death—such as an enjoyable job or a treasured friendship—we don't know *how* to mourn. How can we, when we haven't wept even for the greatest of sorrows: death. Americans don't often become sad or sorrowful. More frequently, we just feel angry and frustrated. A good dose of mourning might really help to clear out our spiritual pipes!

Augustine learned his lesson and took to heart his obligation to pray for his mother's eternal destiny. Listen to his final plea on Monica's behalf:

Thus, God of my heart, my glory and my life, leaving aside for a time my mother's good deeds for which I give thanks to you in joy, I now pray to you for my mother's sins. Grant my prayer through that true medicine of our prayers, Jesus Christ, who hung upon the cross and who is now sitting at your right hand to make intercession for us. For I know that she dealt mercifully and from her heart and forgave those who trespassed against her. Do you also then forgive such trespasses as she may have been guilty of in the years since her baptism. Forgive them I beseech you and enter not into judgment with her.

Let your mercy be exalted above your justice for your words are true and you have promised that the merciful shall attain mercy. I believe, O Lord, that you have already granted what I am asking. But let him not be offended, O Lord, at the things my mouth would utter, for on the day when my mother's death was so close she was not concerned that her body should be wrapped beautifully or embalmed with spices, nor gave any thought to choosing a monument or burial in her own country. Of such things she gave my brother and I no command.

She asked only one thing, that we would remember our mother every day at the altar of God which she served without ever missing so much as a single day on which she knew that holy victim was offered, by whom the handwriting is blotted out of that decree which is against us, by which offering the enemy is overcome and in whom we are conquerors. To this sacrament of our redemption my mother, your handmaid, had bound her soul by the bond of faith.

Let nothing wrest her from your protection. Let neither the lion nor the dragon bar her way by force or craft for she will not answer at the judgment that she owes nothing lest she should be contradicted by that cunning accuser. But she will answer that her debts had been remitted by him to whom no one can ever hand back the price which he paid though he owed it not. And so let my mother rest in peace with her husband.[2]

How exquisite are these words, how filled with faith and true mourning. We know from history that Augustine was comforted in his loss, that he was blessed in his mourning, and that he finally left behind his tears on Monica's behalf. And because God had comforted him, Augustine was able to extend comfort to many others in need. Indeed, this great saint went on to spend the rest of his life drying the tears of many other believers.

## BEING IN THE KNOW

While in the midst of mourning, we sometimes feel as if we have fallen into a huge black hole from which we will never emerge. But mourning is a wound gradually healed by faith. We must grieve the loss of family, friends, jobs, causes—of all the good things in our lives that come to an end.

Scripture tells us that Jesus himself mourned the death of Lazarus. Even though he knew his friend would soon be restored to life, the loss was very real. A loved one had suffered and died—"fallen asleep," as he termed it. Mary and Martha grieved the loss of their brother, even though they themselves believed in the resurrection. "When Jesus saw her [Mary] weeping, and the Jews who came with her also weeping, he was deeply moved in spirit and troubled; and he said, 'Where have you laid him?' They said to him, 'Lord, come and see.' Jesus wept" (Jn 11:33-35).

Our lives are filled with little deaths—perhaps the alienation of close relatives or dear friends, the failure of a life's work, the frustration of a valued project or goal. Many of us go into our later years covered with scars and even open wounds. Yet each loss can teach us a critical lesson of the spiritual life: we have here no lasting city but seek one that is to come. This is hardly a popular message to this generation but it is as true as ever. Every little death brings us one step closer to understanding the real meaning of life.

In this way, St. Augustine linked the Spirit's gift of knowledge to the Beatitude of mourning. Knowledge is a gift which helps us to know, at a very deep level, what life is all about. With the aid of this gift, we begin to know even as we are known by God himself.

Sometimes knowledge speaks thunderously, as it did at the grave of Lazarus when his sister Martha proclaimed, "I know that he will rise again in the resurrection on the last day" (Jn 11:24). Sometimes it whispers to us in the wake of a serious loss, "All is well; I am here." As the gift of knowledge operates in us, the Holy Spirit teaches us lessons so vast that no written word can encompass them—lessons about life and death, time and eternity.

One of the most important lessons of life is about death. Like the wooden hoop around an embroidery project, our allotted number of years provides the frame of life. Death puts our pilgrimage on this earth into perspective, makes it measurable, comprehensible, even endurable. How awful if we could never leave this world! Yet in our time, death has been cheapened and trivialized by the endless phony deaths on television, the uncountable deaths of the innocent and unborn, the sterilized deaths in hospitals.

People in our day have no awe of death; consequently, they have no awe of life. We need the Spirit's gift of knowledge to help us see every moment of this earthly journey as a precious preparation for knowing our Heavenly Comforter.

The popular expression "being in the know" refers to someone who knows something about which others are ignorant.

Those who make use of the gift of knowledge are the people really "in the know." The Spirit himself teaches us what life is all about—a kind of knowledge we can't find in books or in school. Many illiterate people living in remote places know what life is about—that it passes away, and that somehow the good we do accompanies us beyond the doors of death. Many learned people fail to grasp this knowledge and even belittle those who have it.

Do not wait for a time of death or loss to ask for this gift of knowledge, this ability to know things not as they appear but as they really are. Like all the other gifts of the Holy Spirit, this knowledge is radically available to all who are baptized and who try to live an authentic Christian life.

And if you have this gift, do not let yourself become confused through worldliness and lack of spiritual understanding. Use the light that is so readily available and act accordingly. Those who are overly attached to this world are not merely naïve; they are stupid. May God so sift us that the chaff in our lives cannot lead us astray.

~

*O wisest of teachers and Enlightener of all minds, I ask you, Holy Spirit, to continue to teach me even when I don't want to learn. From you only good can come because you are goodness itself. And you teach me so much in times of sorrow and loss. You who are the pure light of all being can teach me so much in what to me seems darkness and injustice. I fear the shadows of the future and dread more days of sorrow and yet as I look back I have learned so much from you in the dark times. Give your comfort to all who seek you and to all who have lost sight of you but who nevertheless call out in their darkness. For the shadows will someday fall away and in your light we shall see light. Amen.*

# CHAPTER 4

# *The Second Beatitude of Purification: Hounded for the Kingdom*

*Blessed are those who are persecuted for righteousness' sake, for theirs is the kingdom of heaven.*

When I consider the Beatitude of persecution for righteousness' sake, I immediately think of St. Paul. He regularly suffered at the hands of those outside and even inside the Church. He was mocked, reviled, imprisoned, beaten, stoned, and finally beheaded. Clearly, Paul was persecuted for the sake of Christ.

How did this battered disciple react to all his trials? Paul boasted of his own weakness: "Three times I have been ship-wrecked; a night and a day I have been adrift at sea; on frequent journeys, in danger from rivers, danger from robbers, danger from my own people, danger from Gentiles, danger in the city, danger in the wilderness, danger at sea, danger from false brethren; in toil and hardship, through many a sleepless night, in hunger and thirst, often without food, in cold and exposure. And, apart from other things, there is the daily pressure upon me of my anxiety for all the churches" (2 Cor 11:25b-28).

Paul let suffering accomplish its intended effect: to purge his soul so that he could draw nearer to God. Perhaps he was one of the most blessed among us because of his extraordinary sufferings.

Not only did Paul allow his personal suffering to strengthen his own spiritual life, he also drew upon it to encourage those who were younger in the Lord. Consider how Paul described his suffering to Timothy: "Now you have observed my teaching, my conduct, my aim in life, my faith, my patience, my love, my steadfastness, my persecutions, my sufferings, what befell me at Antioch, at Iconium, and at Lystra, what persecutions I endured; yet from them all the Lord rescued me. Indeed all who desire to live a godly life in Christ Jesus will be persecuted" (2 Tm 3:10-12).

Then Paul goes on to speak about his sure reward: "For I am already on the point of being sacrificed; the time of my departure has come. I have fought the good fight, I have finished the race, I have kept the faith. Henceforth there is laid up for me the crown of righteousness, which the Lord, the righteous judge, will award to me on that Day, and not only to me but also to all who have loved his appearing" (2 Tm 4:6-8).

The eighth Beatitude expresses the same truth: those who suffer persecution for the cause of righteousness are blessed because the kingdom of heaven is theirs. In Matthew's Gospel Christ repeats this truth by way of encouraging his disciples. Right after the Beatitudes we read: "Blessed are you when men revile you and persecute you and utter all kinds of evil against you falsely on my account. Rejoice and be glad, for your reward is great in heaven, for so men persecuted the prophets who were before you" (Mt 5:11-12).

## PERSECUTION WITHOUT THE LIONS

Many of us tend to think that persecution went out with the Romans. We automatically equate it with the shedding of blood, like chopping up martyrs or throwing bishops to the lions. While few of us will ever suffer in that way, all of us have been persecuted. The word in Latin is *persequere*, which means "to hound someone." And everyone has been hounded at times.

Has anyone ever gone after you with a vengeance, harassed you until you thought you couldn't take it anymore? Then you have been the object of persecution. It may happen in a work situation when a boss takes out his wrath on anyone who gets in his way. It may take place in the midst of a bitter family dispute. It may be inflicted by a friend who is having an especially bad day. Persecution can even arise in a religious community, among those who have committed themselves to love one another in Christ.

At other times the tables are turned and we ourselves are the persecutors. We are the ones who hound someone because we have some axe to grind. Perhaps we feel that the other person has violated or threatened the "kingdom of me," our own personal fiefdom. Fear prompts retaliation and the battle soon escalates.

This tendency to strike back is part of the human condition. Because of sin, something inside us cries out for revenge and tries to destroy something good. In his spiritual classic, *Markings*, Dag Hammarskjöld said that every one of us has a dark center of evil that makes us rejoice when anything outside the narrowest perspective of our own self-interest suffers defeat.[1]

A famous English writer was reportedly asked, "How do you feel when the critics pan the books of your good friends?" He answered quite honestly, "My heart leaps with joy like a young, wild doe!" Envy and jealousy always lurk just beneath the surface. You may not consent to such feelings; you may not want them; you may be embarrassed by them. But you have to admit they exist!

Because of this dark center of evil within, even the good qualities of others can trigger persecution. Suppose someone sees you coming to church with a bag of food for the poor and snidely remarks, "What are you going to do with that?" When you tell them, the person becomes incensed. "Oh, a little play acting, huh? A little show for the fans? I do believe Good Sam (or Florence Nightingale) lives in our midst."

Usually people don't say such words out loud, but you can guess what's running through their minds. Maybe they cast a glance in your direction and mutter, "A little something for the poor to assuage your conscience? It would take a lot more than a canned ham to get you out of trouble!" Doesn't this kind of thing happen to us? And aren't we on the mud-slinging end of the equation sometimes?

Often, persecution stems from basic prejudice—making a prejudgment or judging without the facts. We rush to judgment because of a person's name or nationality or color or religion, without pausing to check out reality or take a close look at the truth. Or we condemn whole groups of people because of a difficulty or weakness they may have. Somebody says, "I can't stand drunks. I can put up with *anything* but that."

Christ warns us not to judge at all, even if we have what we think are the facts. Yet we continue to fall into this pattern of prejudice. Though our intentions may be fairly benign, such attitudes essentially constitute a little persecution. We toss around labels like "liberal," "conservative," "pre-Vatican II," "post-Vatican II," "radical"—terms which declare our prejudgment concerning someone or some issue.

One person says, "I get sick when I hear about people who like to have Mass in Latin now and then." Others complain, "I hate hearing guitars in church. It's all New Age music." Prejudgment! We all have a right to enjoy whatever we happen to appreciate, as long as it's not sinful. But all sorts of people make up their minds beforehand about what's going to be good for *us*. Or we make up our minds for *them*.

Those of you who have seen me speak at conferences know I always wear the slightly soiled and somewhat disreputable-looking habit of the Franciscans. You can find various rips and spots and a touch of grease now and then on the front. But do you know *why* I always wear my habit? First, it's terribly comfortable. Second, I often travel into dangerous parts of New York City where a habit provides better protection than a bullet-proof vest. A habit also witnesses to the importance of religious faith; it saves a good deal of money on clothes, thereby providing a concrete expression of religious poverty.

But I also get persecuted because of my habit. Some people can't stand religious who wear habits. Others can't stand religious who *don't* wear habits. It all boils down to prejudice or prejudgment.

I remember walking through a park with some of our novices on the way to say morning prayers by the edge of the sea. We suddenly came upon a rather wealthy looking lady, whose face registered shock at seeing eight or nine friars coming out of the woods at six thirty in the morning. She looked up and said, "Are you for real?"

I replied, "I certainly hope so." Although I restrained my barbed tongue, I was actually tempted to say, "Madam, *you* are wearing a wig, false teeth, imitation pearls, cosmetics, and who knows what else. You are about 30 percent artifact yourself. Who are you to question our reality?" I did not say that; it would have been unkind. I am grateful to God that wearing a habit all these years has prepared me for such prejudice.

But I have had prejudiced thoughts too. One time when I was in England I saw a teenage youth with green hair. I became very annoyed. *Why are his parents letting him walk around inflicting his green hair on perfect strangers?* But how would I know why he chose to dye his hair green? Perhaps he was an actor. Or another Augustine on his way to a profound conversion. I have no way of knowing. Maybe he was a budding St. Paul in the throes of adolescence. Members of the early Church must have been extremely prejudiced against someone like Saul of Tarsus, a Jew who was going around killing them "for the sake of righteousness," out of a sincere but mistaken understanding of the will of God. Little did any of them know that this dedicated persecutor of Christians would someday write so much of the New Testament. Don't be too quick to rush to judgment.

## THE PROVISO

The eighth Beatitude's promise of blessing in the face of persecution rests on a clearly stated proviso. It lies sandwiched in the middle like a slice of salami in between two pieces of bread: in order to be blessed, we have to be doing something for the sake of righteousness. It's not enough to avoid our own prejudices and prejudgments; we are also called to work actively for the cause of righteousness in the world.

One of the most obvious righteous causes in the United States at this time is the defense of life. But this is not a popular cause at the moment. Many public officials at even the highest levels of government have changed their views on abortion practically overnight. Defenseless creatures who were viewed as human infants one day may be seen as polliwogs the next under the pressures of political expediency.

Given the current climate, those who defend life are subject to widespread attack. As someone who occasionally attends pro-life demonstrations, I can say that I have never once seen any demonstrators fight back. Often they are cursed and insulted, their dedication to God is vilified and their religion blasphemed, but I have never seen them fight back. I know that once in a while some deranged person does react in violence—to the total disappointment of the pro-life movement. But the clearly stated rule is to resist passively, to not fight back and not answer back.

Ask yourself: do I suffer persecution? Why? Is it for the cause of righteousness? Is it on account of Jesus Christ? That is the big question. If we suffer as a result of our *own* wrongdoing, then we are simply getting our just reward.

What does righteousness mean? Whatever is right in this world is simply a reflection of the goodness and kindness and truth of God. Righteousness is rooted in the very being of God. Goodness which rests on any other foundation will quickly fade away like the morning fog with the first heat of day.

Scripture tells us that not one of us is righteous, that we all behave in ways contrary to the will and thoughts of God (see Romans 3). Certain aspects of our lives must be cleansed and purified. And so we can learn to accept persecution and penance as a means to this goal. King David accepted the insults and humiliation of Shimei for this very reason, observing that perhaps God had inspired this man to speak against him because of his sins (2 Sm 16:5-13).

There is another reason to endure persecution with patience. Righteousness often pertains to human rights, but it ultimately concerns the *rights of God*. Our Creator has ordained that society practice justice and mercy, kindness to the poor and those in need. Therefore, if you wish to grow in the spiritual life, you dare not neglect righteousness, nor pursue it in an unrighteous way.

A number of years ago I had an opportunity to meet Martin Luther King, Jr. Not once that day did I hear him pronounce judgment on his enemies. This was true of all his speeches, I later discovered. This man so deeply committed to the cause of civil rights expressed no condemnation or personal disapproval for those who opposed his cause. He just wasn't that type of person.

Even though Dr. King firmly disagreed with the actions of

his enemies, he could sit patiently in a segregated restaurant somewhere in the Deep South, while some bigot poured a bowl of sugar over his head. Rather than take the insult personally, Dr. King silently took the abuse because he knew that he was working for the cause of righteousness and justice. The newsreels which reported this particular act of persecution and the expression on his face—patient, yet profoundly disapproving—probably did more for the civil rights movement than many of the speeches he gave.

Too many times in history Christians have tried to be Christians in decidedly unchristian ways. But you don't produce the fruit of righteousness by behaving unrighteously. You don't promote peace by being violent. You don't further justice by being unjust. Scripture clearly tells us that the kingdom of God is to be inherited by those who are righteous and who act righteously.

## REVERENCE—THE FORGOTTEN GIFT

As I discussed in the previous chapter, the two Beatitudes of mourning and patient suffering under persecution are the tools God uses to rid our hearts of all that must eventually end up on the trash heap. They reveal the wood, hay, and stubble in our souls. God wants to cleanse us of all that is unholy, of all the positive affections that hold us back. He wants to leave us with only the pure gold of holiness which leads to eternal life.

If we aren't so cleansed by the end of our days, then we will have to pass through the ultimate purification beyond death, which we call purgatory. We will then have to mourn and suffer to make up for what was lacking during our pilgrimage on this earth. So rejoice and be glad for whatever opportunities you do have to mourn and suffer persecution. Great is your reward, and shortened is your stay in the foyer of heaven.

St. Augustine, you will recall, joins this eighth Beatitude

with the first Beatitude on being poor in spirit. Both require the forgotten gift—reverence or fear of the Lord.[2] St. Paul, warning us against unbelief, admonishes us not to become proud but to stand in awe (Rom 11:20). Reverence, a most ennobling quality of human beings, calls us to a relationship of awe with God. It is our great dignity to stand in awe before his might and goodness.

In the Jewish and the Christian Scriptures, reverence—a profound reverence for God—is the moral imperative that requires the persecuted to stand fast for God without blaspheming or appearing to renounce their faith. This is the great moral challenge of martyrdom, of confessing faith. But persecution is also the occasion of the gift of reverence. The person suffering persecution is lifted up by a great awareness of the transcendent majesty of God.

It is interesting, by the way, to see a growing (and most welcome) sense of respect for the environment, which is indeed a gift of God. This awareness should lead to a greater reverence for human life, his most precious gift. It should call us to have the greatest respect for God, for his laws and his call to union with him. In time this will open us, as it did the martyrs, to the gift of reverence or fear of the Lord.

## THE GIFT OF WISDOM, THE WAY OF PROMISE

We see how this Beatitude relates to the glorious deeds of the martyrs. But how does it apply to us poor plodders along the first way of the spiritual life? Can it be that wisdom is necessary even at the beginning, when a person is being cleansed of all voluntary faults and failings?

Whether we have been nominal Christians or enthusiastic ones, we begin this phase of purification after some sudden experience of enlightenment. Once we hear God's call to begin the spiritual journey, we become aware of inner conflict. Like

Augustine, we recognize that we are "at war with ourselves against ourselves." This painful awareness brings suffering. But the conflict is resolved and we begin to surrender to God and the law of the Spirit within. Then we realize that we are in conflict with many people and things as well. We are often misunderstood, even by those close to us. The Prince of Peace, paradoxically, is quoted as saying, "I have not come to bring peace, but a sword... to set a man against his father, and a daughter against her mother" (Mt 10:34, 35). As time goes on, we will have to make many sacrifices and give up much that we hold dear.

We will be misunderstood even by fellow strugglers along the way. Those in the early stages of the spiritual journey often prove to be hostile critics—even, in some sense, enemies of their fellow pilgrims. Such are the pervasive effects of original sin.

In the early stages of our spiritual journey, we must be able to look up and grasp at least vaguely—by means of the gift of wisdom—the promise of God's kingdom. Otherwise we simply will not be able to go on. For this reason, the Fathers of the Church always saw martyrdom as the clearest embodiment of the spiritual life. And they consistently warned believers that following the way of Christ would bring some elements of martyrdom into their lives.


MOURNING AND SUFFERING:
A FRIEND SHOWS THE WAY

Although it happened many years ago, I clearly remember the phone call that informed me of Cardinal Terence Cooke's pending death. At first I was unbelieving; then I was annoyed; then I quickly realized that I must pray.

Those of us who knew Cardinal Cooke well were all plunged into mourning. We were soon to lose a revered and respected archbishop, a public leader who constantly tried to defend the faith and Catholic morality in the world, a gentle man who could make friends with all, even his opponents. We were also about to lose someone who had been a friend and a father to many of us. How could we let him go?

The day before I myself checked into the hospital for heart surgery, I was privileged to spend the better part of an hour with Cardinal Cooke. We both knew it would be the last time we would see each other in this world. What a bright light those precious moments shed on my own path toward God. With the ravages of leukemia apparent on his frail body, the cardinal was already confined to bed. He looked emaciated; he was in pain, and yet the gentle release of death would not come for another long month. And do you know what I found absolutely incredible? My friend was completely and absolutely at peace.

Jesus told us that the things that are done in secret will come to light someday (Lk 8:17). How vividly we saw this borne out after Cardinal Cooke's death. It was then that we all discovered that this simple man had endeared himself not to thousands, not to tens of thousands, but to hundreds of thousands of people. Why? Because he was concerned about the needs and feelings of everyone he met. When the cardinal did anything, all the t's had to be crossed and the i's dotted, so that no one would feel slighted or left out.

Cardinal Cooke was a great lover of people. He wouldn't dream of leaving a church without greeting everyone as they came out, if at all humanly possible. I once saw him standing in pouring rain with an umbrella over his head shaking hands with those who had come to a Mass for the seventy-fifth anniversary of Fr. Solanus Casey's ordination. The cardinal insisted on greeting everyone, in spite of having recently contracted malaria while visiting an impoverished mission in Africa. In addition, he was struggling with the side effects of the chemotherapy he had been having for years. He obviously didn't feel well that day, yet he smiled and listened when an elderly lady gave him a racing form marked with all her predictions for the next day's winners. The Blessed Mother, she said, had told her that if the cardinal followed her tips and bet ten thousand dollars the next morning, he could make enough to rescue the Catholic school system. In his place, I could not have smiled so kindly.

Cardinal Cooke would have his picture taken with grandmothers and grandchildren. I would hazard a guess that he was kissed by more people than any cardinal who ever lived. At his funeral, people lined up down the streets and around the cathedral, waiting four hours to walk past his casket for half a minute. The hundreds of thousands who participated in some aspect of the cardinal's funeral paid tribute to this man who had spent his life standing hours and hours to greet everyone. The truth about this good and gentle man was indeed preached from the housetops that day.

The cardinal provided a model of righteousness. He had always tried to do the right thing since his youth—as a well-mannered altar boy, a hardworking seminarian, a near-perfect priest. Yet when I saw him a month before he died, he had put everything into the hands of God and was at great peace. Having always been concerned about the media's treatment of the Church, he read no newspaper, watched no television, and listened to no radio from the day he received the word that he was dying. Consequently, he knew almost nothing of the wide outpouring of grief over the news of his terminal illness.

How *did* Cardinal Cooke fill his last days?[3] He made what I would call a thirty-day retreat. Every day he concelebrated Mass and recited the Liturgy of the Hours. Different people read spiritual books to him. He prayed and did his work. He wrote beautiful letters promoting the cause of life, the missions, and peace in Ireland. The cardinal made arrangements for diocesan affairs to be given over to his successor in the best possible order. He prepared for his death not by praying for himself, but by offering every pain, suffering, and indignity to God as a prayer for the Pope, for the Church, and for all those in his diocese.

Cardinal Cooke suffered intensely but he suffered in peace and with a sense of humor. Everyone who came into his presence saw what I saw on my last visit: his total acceptance of God's will. It grew to the fullness of a flower, day by torturous day. His sweet-smelling sacrifice of peace and gratitude remained rooted in absolute confidence in the mercy of God.

Terence Cooke obviously enjoyed being archbishop of New York. But then this man enjoyed every aspect of life. He enjoyed being chaplain of a children's home, being a secretary, being procurator of a seminary. Whatever he did he did very well and delighted in every minute of it. If Terence Cooke had been the third assistant of some inner-city parish and passed his days in utter anonymity, he would have enjoyed that just as well.

His motto as archbishop colored his entire life: *"Fiat voluntas tua."* "Thy will be done." Who would have ever dreamed that these words from the Our Father would serve as a headline in a major New York City newspaper on the day of the cardinal's death? Who would have ever thought that this great city would go into mourning over a humble man of God? But it did. And who would have ever thought that someone who was hanging onto the last thread of life and enduring intense pain would exert the effort to write deeply moving letters for causes that had been entrusted to him as the shepherd of souls?[4]

During those last weeks of Cardinal Cooke's life, the fiery illness of leukemia burned away all the chaff and left only the grain to be gathered into the barn. This offering to God was purified with humility and simplicity, without any fanfare or pretense at all. Rest assured that it isn't easy to remain humble when you're a bishop, much less a cardinal. It isn't easy to remain plain and simple when important people of the world come to visit you and write to you in your illness. But Cardinal

Cooke had lived this way all his life, and he persisted in humility to the end.

Blessed are those who mourn and blessed are those who weep. And so we mourned and we wept. Many tears were shed at Cardinal Cooke's passing, and not only by his close associates. I saw one letter from a distinguished public figure of New York City, himself not a member of the Catholic faith, and who in fact had often been on the opposite side of issues to which the cardinal was deeply dedicated. This man's farewell was written in longhand and read in part:

> Your Eminence,
> I have learned with great sorrow of your illness, and although we have occasionally had our disagreements, I want you to know that in the twenty years I have been your friend, I have always considered you my spiritual guide.

The cardinal's funeral was attended by not only his friends but also his opponents, not only those who agreed with his causes but also those who were deeply committed to the opposite side. It was a tribute to the cardinal's efforts to represent as best as he could the presence of Jesus Christ to the diverse inhabitants of a vast metropolis.

As I mourned the loss of my friend and spiritual leader, I was comforted. Why? Because I believe that he received the reward of righteousness: what eye has not seen, what ear has not heard, and what the heart cannot conceive—what God has prepared for those who love him (1 Cor 2:9). Blessed are they who are hounded for righteousness' sake, for the kingdom of heaven is theirs. And Terence Cooke had frequently suffered persecution at the hands of his critics.

The day I said my final farewell, the cardinal's last words to me about his persecutors were brief: "Benedict, they just didn't understand. They didn't mean it. They just didn't understand. It was my fault, I did not make myself clear."

Tears filled my eyes as I stumbled out the door. I could hear an unspoken prayer coming from his tiny room, so poorly furnished, so plain: "Father, forgive them, for they did not understand." The cardinal could offer that prayer with all his heart, because wisdom had given him an insight, a mysterious knowledge, of the glorious inheritance that awaited him.

*Let me be in reverence of your majesty and greatness and let me be in silent awe of your mysterious being and endless days. But most of all, Holy Spirit, let my reverence be like that of a child for his parents. Let me have the reverence toward you that loving spouses have for each other. Let me walk in silence in the beauty of your creation and see the fingerprints of your majesty on the sky and in the earth. Let me be deeply moved by your beauty when I see it on the face of a child and let me be most compassionate when I see your wisdom etched over a face marked with suffering. O Holy Spirit, give me your gift of reverence that I may always pass through life in a certain silent awe, knowing that you will have passed over the darkness and emptiness of the void and called it to life and that you call me to a more loving life in this world and to eternity in the next. Amen.*

# CHAPTER 5

# The Third Beatitude of Purification: Soul Food

*Blessed are those who hunger and thirst for righteousness, for they shall be safisfied.*

"*M*r. Rodriguez," I asked, "Why did you ever come to New York City?"

He answered, "So that my children might have a chance."

I was sitting in the middle of an absolutely wretched hovel given to him by the welfare department when he arrived from Puerto Rico. His native land provided little health care for the poor—not good news for a man of little means who had been diagnosed as having a serious heart ailment. In need of medical assistance and a new start, the whole family had packed up their meager belongings and come to New York.

Generations ago, most of our ancestors came to America for the same reasons. Immigrants from England, Ireland, Germany, Poland, Italy, and other European countries packed whatever they could take on board ship. Many fled oppression in their homeland with nothing but the clothes on their backs.

After they had braved the rolling seas for several weeks, these desperate voyagers passed through Ellis Island with a new gleam of hope in their eyes. Willing to toil for twelve or fourteen hours a day for pennies, most of them went to work as soon as they got off the boat. Why? So that their descendants could have a chance for a better life. These brave souls endured hunger and thirst not out of greed but for the sake of justice. Do those of us who enjoy a better life because of their sacrifice ever remember them?

Do we ever stop to think of the soldiers who fought in the American Revolution to gain our freedom? Off the little island of Manhattan, fifteen hundred American soldiers were imprisoned in ships and left to die of starvation and foul diseases like scurvy. How much better to die gloriously in battle! Yet because of the sacrifices of such unsung patriots, Americans enjoy a democratic society with considerable rights compared to citizens in many other lands.

We also enjoy another invaluable inheritance. Whether your ancestors were converted almost two thousand years ago or a thousand years ago or a hundred years ago, they received the gift of faith because of those who made hunger and thirst their constant companions in order to spread the gospel. Our knowledge of the saving grace of Christ is a wondrous gift, but our awareness of his teaching comes to us only because others endured hardship for our sake—people like the apostles, the missionaries who brought the gospel to Europe fifteen hundred years ago, and those who brought the gospel to America.

In fact, the whole world would be a terrible jungle, a dark forest with no hope, were it not for those who hungered and thirsted for righteousness. And we don't have to look so long ago to find some of them. People of many different religions and nationalities have struggled through our own so-called "enlightened century"—a time of war, terror, economic enslavement, and unjust imprisonment. Stories of the heroic martyrs of the Holocaust move us to tears: Edith Stein, St. Maximilian Kolbe, the Swedish diplomat Raoul Wallenberg, the little Jewish girl Anne Frank, and all those who lost their lives for the sake of righteousness.

Even though the Iron Curtain has fallen, its evil effects continue to haunt countries decimated by decades of injustice. Even as I write, large numbers of innocent people still suffer poverty and injustice in South America, Central America, Northern Ireland, the Near East, the Middle East, China, Africa, Bosnia, and elsewhere.

Why do they struggle? For righteousness. Their trials become all the more painful because well-intentioned zealots can be found on both sides. The great tragedy in most wars is that people of good will go about killing other people of good will. If they only knew their adversaries personally, most of them would never be able to lift a finger against them. How strange and how heartbreaking.

## WHAT DOES IT MEAN TO HUNGER AND THIRST?

Although poverty, homelessness, and starvation certainly exist in our country, most Americans don't have much personal experience with going hungry for any length of time. No matter how hungry you are, McDonald's is not far away. Even if you decide to fast all day, the refrigerator continues to hum in the kitchen. And when you're thirsty, you can usually find a nearby drinking fountain.

Just the knowledge that relief is close at hand makes any suffering more endurable. It's like a lady I know who loves living in New York because of the theater and ballet, yet she hardly ever goes anywhere. When I asked her about this, she said, "I just *feel* better because I know it's there." A well-stocked refrigerator in the next room provides the same kind of solace.

First-century Israel lacked such comforts. Our Lord was speaking to peasants who knew firsthand what hunger and thirst meant. As a little boy growing up in Nazareth, Jesus no doubt walked down to the well in the morning, filled up an animal-skin flask, and brought it home to his family. Water was a very precious commodity in such a dry climate. Unfortunate travelers died of thirst in the desert. Beasts were poisoned by brackish water during periods of drought and perished.

The poor also knew hunger intimately. If they were driven to steal, the county dungeon offered no mess hall where they could line up to have an aluminum tray filled with something edible. Unless concerned relatives brought them something to eat, prisoners simply starved to death.

How can those of us who live in a land of plenty begin to know what it means to hunger and thirst? One way is by denying ourselves enough physical comfort to create an inner vacuum, a hole which can be filled only by God.

Those who seek to grow in the spiritual life must know this burning hunger and thirst, and then not complain about it. If you feel this pain because of the destructive world around you, then live with it. If the pain is for someone you care about, then allow the hunger and thirst for righteousness to be a sharp and steady pain that will spur you to pray for that person every day. If you're bothered by the wretched society in which we live—the iniquitous anti-culture that spews out garbage and drugs to mere children—then hunger and thirst for righteousness. Only then will God deliver us.


THE FATTED CALF

Christ promises that those who hunger and thirst for righteousness shall be satisfied. But the scriptural term "satisfied" doesn't mean what we think. This Beatitude really says, "How full of bliss are those who hunger and thirst for righteousness for they shall be *stuffed* or completely satisfied."[1]

Think about what it means to be "stuffed." Even the most temperate Christians go back for seconds at Thanksgiving dinner, heaping their plates with an extra portion of green beans almondine, luscious creamed pearl onions, or juicy turkey breast with stuffing. Some of us may even go back for thirds (and fourths), and not necessarily for the vegetables and salads. Then we fret about the calorie count.

I doubt the saints had so died to self that they never said, "Please pass the hors d'oeuvres." When St. Francis lay on his death bed, he asked a woman called Fra Jacapona to make him some marzipan candies. He is one of the few saints who died eating sweets, despite the fact that he was a great penitent.

If you grew up in an immigrant home that practiced customs from the old country, you could be as poor as church mice all year long, but nonetheless feast on a major holiday. A few years ago an Italian family invited me for Thanksgiving dinner. We started with prosciutto and antipasto and other hors d'oeuvres. We proceeded to work our way through the pasta dishes and the rolitini and the Italian meatballs. We certainly had plenty to eat, but I chuckled to myself, *this will be my first turkeyless Thanksgiving*. Then, to my absolute horror, after all of this food, the hostess proceeded to bring in the turkey and all the trimmings. They had two major meals! Do you know why? Because peasants in Italy long ago knew what it was to be hungry. On major holidays—or *holy days*—they found a way to celebrate. "They shall be stuffed."

I knew many old immigrant Jews when I was growing up. No matter how poor they were, Jewish families would clean the house, light candles, and feast on the Sabbath. Gentile boys in our neighborhood would turn on the oven for the Orthodox Jews so that they could prepare their food without doing any forbidden work. *They shall be satisfied.* And when we boys received our tip at sundown to buy a candy bar, so were we.

*When* shall we be completely satisfied? *When* shall we be stuffed? Don't expect it to happen in this world. We hunger and thirst for what lies beyond us. And if you do turn out to be one of those rare and chosen souls who hunger and thirst for justice and happen to get it, cheer up! God will bless you with more crosses of another kind. Don't ever be lulled into thinking that the Lord is going to let you get away with a whole life filled with the abundance of Thanksgiving. In my own experience, those who seek God more often experience life like an overcast Tuesday evening in Lent with cold leftovers on the table. But it doesn't have to be that way.

I remember traveling with a missionary deep into a Louisiana bayou, driving along pebbly dirt roads to visit a Creole family who lived in a small cabin. The walls were decorated with the kind of flotsam and jetsam a department store would discard after Christmas. A bit of this and a bit of that, none of which went together at all. As we walked up the path lined with little painted stones, I could see that the tiny house was neat and clean.

Yet this man and wife who had so little in the way of worldly possessions were filled with gratitude to God. "Father, we are so grateful for everything we have received," they said to me. Grateful for what? For practically nothing. *They shall be satisfied.*

You and I might argue that these parents were too passive, that they should have fought for their rights, at least for the sake of their sons and daughters. But they chose not to fight. And their children received from them a strength that permitted them to go north and find what they deemed a better life.

Some of their children worked for the federal government in Washington. The proud parents displayed a newspaper picture of their son who had achieved a significant award. Where did this next generation get the courage to fight against injustice and to make their own way in an unkind world? From these brave and humble souls who had scratched out a meager existence on the pebble road, the husband and wife who were so grateful to God for all he had given them. To you and me, it would have been nothing. Blessed are they.

# FIGHTING THE GOOD FIGHT

Are you grateful for those who have struggled to make *your* world less of a jungle? Are you willing to suffer for the sake of righteousness in your own life? Your struggle may be external, as in the fight for civil rights or for the rights of the unborn. Or it may be an internal struggle: bending your will to the will of God, bowing your heart to his rights and those of your fellow creatures.

Whether your struggle is visible or hidden, the Holy Spirit wants to give you courage to go beyond your frightened self. God himself promises to carry you along by his own power whenever you have lost the will to fight.

The Beatitudes will strengthen us as we struggle for righteousness in all the circumstances of our lives, even the most ordinary ones. For example, we sometimes endure hardship simply because of where we live. I myself suffer a little for righteousness just by living in a densely populated, unsafe area of New York City. Someone once said to me, "Aren't you frightened about going on a pilgrimage to Israel?" Believe me, if you're not frightened about living in New York, you can't be frightened about going to Israel. In many respects, the latter may be a lot safer. In the five blocks from our friary to the subway, I regularly pass by two graffiti memorials to youngsters gunned down in the street.

Perhaps you have suffered for the sake of someone dear to you, some relative or friend who needs to know more of God's love. Perhaps you have offered your own pain as a prayer on someone else's behalf. Keep it up! But don't expect to see immediate results. In fact, you and I will likely depart from this earth still praying for some of our family members who are far away from God.

Those who hunger and thirst for righteousness frequently fail to see what they long for. This is not what the media leads us to expect. The ongoing struggle for justice in America has been boiled down to televised episodes of thirty or sixty minutes (minus an onslaught of commercials) in which the good guys always win. Two-hour movies manage to untangle monstrous problems. Real life is much more complex.

## THE GIFT OF COURAGE

People occasionally comment that Pope John Paul II looks so serious and burdened at papal audiences, while at other times he appears very enthusiastic. Many pilgrims are puzzled by this contrast. Stop to think about how today's headlines affect you. Then consider that the Holy Father probably often hears the bad news before it ever hits the media. In a recent meeting with a group of American bishops, the Holy Father greeted them with the simple but revealing word, "Courage."

Not many of us will be called upon to carry the tremendous burdens of the pope, but we all need the gift of courage in our quest for righteousness. Courage comes in big bites and little bites, whatever we need to overcome our own personal obstacles. But first we have to be hungry enough to ask for it.

In English, the word "courage" usually connotes the ability to stand up in the midst of a particular danger. But in the Romance languages, it suggests a whole attitude toward life—a certain enthusiastic or at least persistent determination in the face of all obstacles. The latter definition is closer to the meaning of this marvelous gift of the Holy Spirit which gives us the strength to face even the most difficult challenges of life.

Courage is a natural human quality, which by grace can be raised to a Christian virtue. It is also a gift of the Holy Spirit which enables us to endure much for the kingdom of God— even if we aren't exactly courageous people. The virtue of courage can make a brave person good (and not all of them are), but the gift of the Holy Spirit, the gift of courage, can even make a cowardly person brave. And aren't many of us cowards at heart?

English often uses the words "courage" and "fortitude" interchangeably. But Fr. Andrew Apostoli, in his instructive book *The Gift of God, The Holy Spirit*, makes a helpful distinction. Fortitude gives us the patience to endure things, he points out. It is a patient strength in the midst of adversity. Courage, on the other hand, is a quality of mind and heart that enables us to encounter difficulties and dangers with firmness and without fear.[2] In fact, both these are largely found in the gift of the Holy Spirit: patient endurance in trial and tireless activity in overcoming dangers and weariness.

## DO WE DARE LOOK WITHIN?

Have you ever gathered the courage to peek into your own soul? I don't know about you, but I am appalled when I look into mine. How little it cares for the rights of God, how far away it still tarries from his sovereignty. This realization challenges me not to be afraid to hunger and thirst for personal sanctity.

Words from a sermon by Cardinal John Henry Newman have given me much to think about when I look into that weedy patch I call my soul.

The aim of most men, esteemed, conscientious, and religious, or who are at least what is called honorable, upright men, is, to all appearances, not how to please God but how to please themselves without displeasing him.... They make this world the object of their minds and use religion as a corrective, a restraint, upon too much attachment to this world. They think that religion is a negative thing, a sort of moderate love of the world, a moderate luxury, a moderate avarice, a moderate ambition, a moderate selfishness.... You see this in the course of trade, of public life, of literature, in all matters where men have objects to pursue. You see it in religious activities, in which it too commonly happens that the chief aim is to attain by any means a certain definite end, religious in deed, but of man's own choosing; not to please God.[3]

Our Lord preached hunger and thirst for the righteousness that is within. He wasn't much interested in the external righteousness of those who were known as "honorable men." If we don't have righteousness within, then we will never be able to bring righteousness to the world outside of us.

Only grace enables us to carry out this call. Only with the gifts of the Holy Spirit can we move anything in our world toward righteousness—including ourselves. The Holy Spirit must guide and push us, even dragging our weary bodies along the right path.

Jesus saw great injustices everywhere he went, yet he never launched a civil rights campaign. Instead, he focused his concern almost exclusively on inner righteousness. Our Lord knew that only a radical change within the heart and soul of one person at a time would eventually bring about the end of slavery and the decline of the pagan Roman Empire. In fact, most of the civil rights we enjoy today can be traced to the preaching of the Hebrew prophets and the preaching of the gospel, the good news of salvation.

Christ addressed his teaching primarily to the poor and the outcasts of his day. He spent his time with those who had been deprived of their human rights and were trying to survive, to scratch out a meager living in the midst of a difficult world. Whenever Jesus did confront the temporal powers, he soundly rebuked them for abusing the poor.

Our Lord himself was one of the poor, one who dared to rock the boat. As such he was persecuted by the Sadducees and the Pharisees, the ruling religious elite in Jewish society who represented, respectively, the ultra-liberals and the ultra-conservatives. But while those in power typically found fault with Jesus, the poor usually understood and accepted him.

Unless Jesus comes again in our lifetime, you and I will go down into our graves in a world still saturated with violence and injustice. If the earth is a slightly better place because of our generation, we won't be able to tell.

Perhaps we really do live in singularly immoral times, dangerous times where great numbers of human beings are woefully misused and abused. In all honesty, I find nothing in the daily newspapers to convince me that this particular century represents any great advance over the days of cave dwellers. This is after all the century of holocausts: the Armenians in 1916; the Ukrainians in the 1930s; the Jews before and during the Second World War; and more recently the Cambodians and the Somalians and the Bosnians. If we went on to include other atrocities—like those of death squads in Latin America—would the list ever end?

## A GLIMPSE OF RIGHTEOUSNESS

Held captive in the midst of such a wretched world, how can we possibly glimpse the righteousness for which we should hunger and thirst? Yet it does glimmer here and there throughout history. For example, I find sparks of heroic virtue in the Greek tragedies. Written by creative geniuses, stories such as Homer's *Iliad* or Aeschylus' *Oresteia* are much more than tales of unparalleled disasters and sorrows without hope; they also tell of people who show great courage. Perhaps the most touching is the story of the little princess, Iphigenia.

Agamemnon, king of Mycenae, gathered the Greek forces for an expedition against Troy. But the goddess Artemis refused to send the favorable winds necessary for the army to set sail. The king had offended her, and only the sacrifice of his daughter would appease the goddess. Like the daughter of Jepthah in the Book of Judges, Iphigenia voluntarily went to her death. The king met death too: on his return he was murdered by his wife Clytemnestra and her lover. And later, his own death was avenged by his son Orestes and his daughter Electra. Human nobility as well as human weakness are revealed in these tragic characters from twenty-five hundred years ago.

The Jewish Scriptures too give many accounts of those who hungered for righteousness. Unlike the characters of Greek drama, however, they also received a glimpse of eternal life. Elijah the prophet is a prime example, along with the seven sons in the Book of Maccabees who died while their mother encouraged them to remain faithful.

We also catch a glimmer of the reward of righteousness when we read about Christian martyrs. St. Stephen cried out as he was martyred, "Behold, I see the heavens opened, and the Son of man standing at the right hand of God" (Acts 7:56). He beheld with his own eyes the fulfillment of the promised resurrection. Ever so briefly, this man of faith held heaven in his hands as he passed on to life everlasting.

The disciples who saw Jesus transfigured also beheld something of the reward of righteousness. But Jesus instructed them as they descended from the Mount of Transfiguration to "tell no one the vision, until the Son of Man is raised from the dead" (Mt 17:9). Even those who had been his constant companions couldn't understand what it meant to "rise from the dead." Yet Jesus allowed them to glimpse the glorious reward of a life given over to hunger and thirst for righteousness.

Martyrs in our own time offer us an inkling of this righteousness for which we are to hunger and thirst. Blessed Edith Stein wrote this testimony from the concentration camp: "So far I have been able to pray gloriously."[4] St. Maximilian Kolbe encouraged his fellow inmates who were suffering deprivation, torture, and death in a concentration camp not to hate their guards but to love them and to pray for their conversion.[5]

When Christians hunger and thirst for righteousness, they receive, in some mysterious way, a foretaste of the goodness of

God. If you want to grow spiritually, if you want your life to have meaning, if you want the crosses and vicissitudes you encounter to be a blessing not only to you but to others, then you must learn the meaning of this Beatitude. Ask the Holy Spirit to help you and he will.


## TILLING THE SOIL AROUND US

Inner righteousness cannot help but cry out on behalf of others who are being abused or misused. Are you personally interested in the rights of those around you? When someone in your family, neighborhood, or parish is treated unjustly in some way—even accidentally or by someone who may be poorly informed—are you able to calmly and quietly speak up on this person's behalf, even if those words cost you dearly?

When you are the one who is doing the persecuting, even inadvertently, are you willing to repent? If it is quietly (or not so quietly) brought to your attention, do you have enough humility to admit, "All right, I was wrong. I'll retrace my steps. I'll reconsider that course of action"?

Do you take an interest in the spiritual, psychological, and material welfare of your neighbor who doesn't even know you? Are you concerned for the suffering of others? Not long ago I became aware of a man who was being treated inhumanely by those who suspected that he was a homosexual. I have no idea if he was or not. Yet on the basis of a few mannerisms, he was treated rudely and even unjustly.

I agree with the teaching of the Church that homosexual activity is contrary to the Scriptures and to Christian tradition. So are lots of other things that go on in this world in every phase of human behavior. After working for years as a psychologist, I am convinced that the homosexual identity is a misfortune, morally and personally. But does this justify persecuting those who suffer this misfortune? Not at all. Not even if they express anger at the Church for its firm moral stance based on Scripture and Christian tradition.

Alcoholism, drug addiction, and even a chronically sour disposition are all misfortunes that wreak havoc on others. In fact, grouches have probably done more harm to the human race than any other single group! After all, their numbers are greater. But we don't set out to persecute grouches even though their behavior often seriously and habitually violates Christian charity.

So I decided to intervene on behalf of this man who was suspected of being homosexual. As I did, I noticed a raised eyebrow here and a sneer there; I became acutely aware that my actions might cause some to question my judgment. But injustice is injustice no matter who the victim is. I consider irrelevant the fact that I got little or no thanks for my efforts.

Capital punishment is another issue that motivates me to hunger for righteousness. I am convinced that it is an absolute barbarism which cannot be morally justified, and so it troubles me deeply. For example, I was distressed to hear of one man in a Florida state prison who was executed ten years after his crime—which means that he was far different from the person he had been at the time of his crime. In fact, his last words were, "I have no bitterness toward anyone. God bless us all." Considering the length of the appeals process and all the legal hurdles, cases like this are not at all unusual.

A relative of mine happened to hold a significant position in the Florida state prison system. He told me that the vast majority of the people on death row were severely disturbed or totally out of their minds on the day they committed their crimes. Driven by forces beyond their control, they knew little about what they were doing, he said. Even if my relative's remarks were only partially true, what if the law allowed even one innocent person to be executed? That possibility alone should obviate capital punishment.

I recall reading about a man in the state of New York who

was released after many years behind bars. The real culprit had finally confessed to the crime on his deathbed. This person had been imprisoned for most of his life for something he didn't do. I wonder how many innocent individuals have been executed over the years?

I don't personally believe that criminal acts offer any justification for purposely killing another human being. I myself have worked with countless disturbed people and delinquent youngsters, some of whom went on to make a career of serious crime, so I know a lot about what goes into making a criminal. If you probe into their backgrounds, most of these people have endured the ugliest conditions imaginable from their earliest years. And so I believe that human beings have no right to take the lives of other human beings, except in self-defense—and then only if they see no other way to preserve their own life or the life of another innocent person. That seems to me the only possible moral exception.

If we take a stand against death being dealt to others in one form, it seems to me that we must oppose killing in all forms. As the possibility of legislation favoring euthanasia looms over our country, those who believe in God should stand together on a very simple proposition: thou shalt not kill.

As I write these pages the issues of life and the sacredness of human existence loom large in western nations. The great tyrannies of this century, Nazism and Communism, took the lives of the innocent and defenseless with no moral qualms at all. The western nations are now doing the same to the unborn; the severely and chronically ill and the aged are next in line. Where will it stop? That question will be answered rightly only by those who are willing to hunger and thirst for righteousness.

I admit that these are areas where I personally hunger and thirst for justice. You may have a different opinion on some of these issues, or feel strongly about different causes. But I challenge you to ask yourself: What *does* drive you to your knees in prayer? Are you willing to suffer serious inconvenience because of a personal commitment to rectifying some injustice? You cannot continue to grow in the spiritual life unless you pray and work for justice in your own way and in your own sphere of influence. And unless you first hunger and thirst for righteousness, you cannot be satisfied.

## FIGHTING FOR JUSTICE, HARLEM-STYLE

Harlem boasts one of my favorite communities, a group of Franciscan sisters called The Franciscan Handmaids of the Most Pure Heart of Mary. Their foundress, Mother Theodore Williams, was born just three years after the Emancipation Proclamation. Both of her parents had been slaves for much of their lives.

Mother Theodore was baptized as an infant and brought up as a Catholic. In a time when many people questioned whether African-Americans could do such a thing, she joined a community called the Colored Sisters of St. Francis. When that group disbanded, she joined The Oblate Sisters of Providence, a black community still prominent in the United States. She then started the Handmaids of Mary and came to Harlem.

So many years after the heyday of the civil rights movement, most of us might not realize how much courage these women required. After the period called Reconstruction, white Southerners quickly reasserted control of their governments and began passing segregationist legislation. Black Catholics found themselves in an especially difficult position; the vast majority of African-Americans were Protestant, and most post-slavery leaders were ministers.

Nor did white Catholics offer much help. Remember that most American Catholics in those days were immigrants from Europe who had never laid eyes on a black person—with the lone exception of one wise man in the nativity scene. They also tended to be poor themselves, victims of economic depression. And like most ethnic groups, they were terribly clannish. These foreigners all got off the boat together and strained after the same piece of bread.

The desperate struggle for survival kindled deep animosity between the Catholics and Jews, the Poles and the Irish, the Italians and the Irish. And many white Catholics resented the fact that they were drafted into the Civil War to fight slavery the day they got off the boat. They had no idea what the Civil War was all about. They didn't know north from south. In New York City the Irish greeted the draft with riots that created a huge uproar. (Mind you, I'm not reciting some impersonal history lesson here: two of my paternal great-grandfathers fought in the Civil War soon after arriving in the United States.) As the nineteenth century drew to a close, all this smoldering resentment flamed into the racial prejudice of the twentieth century.

Many heroes and heroines arose in the black community during those tumultuous times. Despite severe economic difficulties, these individuals had been graced with unusual talents, strengths which enabled them to rise above the injustice that surrounded them. In 1881, Booker T. Washington was appointed head of the Tuskegee Institute in Alabama, a new school for blacks. Born of slave parents, George Washington Carver went on to direct agricultural research at this same school. Some of these heroic figures were simple folks who preached the gospel. One of my favorites is Sojourner Truth, a black woman who was a slave until 1827, and then went on to preach the gospel, emancipation, and women's rights.·

Mother Theodore was another of these extraordinary individuals who overcame the injustice of the times. God in his providence called her—along with a number of black religious sisters and priests—to combat prejudice by working for righteousness. Mother Theodore's work began when the bishop of Savannah learned about some proposed segregation laws that would make it illegal for white people to teach black students. He decided that he had better prepare some black teachers for the Catholic schools that served black children. Mother Theodore was asked to start a community, and she rose to the challenge.

Thankfully, that law never passed. And so the community that was started in order to combat a potential evil found itself in search of a purpose. It found one when the archbishop of New York invited Mother Theodore and her sisters to work in the city's black schools, beginning with the first black parish, St. Benedict the Moor in Manhattan. As the black population moved into Harlem, the sisters found plenty of work to do. Their mother house is now located in the very center of Harlem.

Try to envision the impossible circumstances Mother Theodore faced. The parishes were so poor that the sisters couldn't earn enough money, not even if they taught all day. So in order to support the order and continue its good work, the Handmaids of Mary took in laundry after school. Can you imagine teaching all day and then coming home and running a laundry for the people in the community, just so that you would have the privilege of teaching their children in school?

In that immense poverty Mother Theodore began still another labor of love: during the Depression she opened a soup kitchen for the poor. The city helped her by dispatching huge loads of cabbage and a few other vegetables and a bit of meat to her convent. But this was Mother Theodore's special project and she herself ladled out the soup. Even when she grew old and too weak to continue, she refused to let someone else take over. An article printed at the time of Mother Theodore's death in 1931 had this to say:

"Please sister, may I have a sandwich?"

The alcoholic who spoke to the sister who answered the door did not know the sister's name, nor did he know that the sandwich he begged would cost her her life. This sister was for the people of Harlem just another of a small group of women God sent to care for them. To the sisters in the convent on West 131st Street she was their Mother Foundress who died from pneumonia, which she contracted feeding the poor because of her own malnutrition.[6]

Mother Theodore literally died caring for the poor. But she wasn't the only religious sister of that period who shone as a beacon for the cause of justice. So did another woman who resembled her hardly at all: Katharine Drexel. Born into one of the wealthiest families in America, this woman harbored one passion: the evangelization of minority groups. She also became a nun and founded the Sisters of the Blessed Sacrament, a group who worked alongside Mother Theodore's Handmaids of Mary.

Mother Katharine Drexel arranged to have her community receive a great deal of money from her family fortune as long as she lived.[7] This income supported a large number of schools and missions to African and Native Americans. It also helped her to found the only black, Catholic university in the United States, Xavier University in New Orleans. Mother Drexel, now beatified, lived well into her nineties, far beyond any of her doctors' predictions. And every year she was alive, the sisters received a ton of money from the family estate. I suspect that Mother Drexel fought to stay alive so that she could see her inheritance filter down to help evangelize the poor she so loved.

Mother Theodore died for the gospel; Mother Drexel stayed alive for the gospel. Both ultimately did the same thing: they hungered and thirsted for justice. Because of their labors, I believe that Mother Theodore and Mother Drexel saw the tops of the mountains, a glimpse of the glory that is to be revealed in the life to come.

I believe that the valiant members in both their communities still catch a glimpse of glory from time to time, but that they more often look out over parched plains at those who hunger and thirst. They walk the dark streets from which hundreds of thousands of youngsters will never escape. They constantly look into lifeless eyes because a person of limited ability perceives no place to go, no way out. These courageous sisters live with that painful reality day in and day out.

Still, as we can see in the lives of people like Mother Theodore, there *is* a way out and a glory to come for those who seek righteousness. Mother Theodore experienced the hunger of deprivation. She met prejudice in the black community because she was Catholic, and in the white community because she was black. And whenever she walked the streets and saw the children who would never manage to climb the narrow ladder out of the ghetto, she knew the far greater hunger and thirst for justice.

When Mother Theodore lay dying in the hot summer of 1931, the sisters could hear her singing to herself all the verses of "O Come All Ye Faithful." It was Christmas in July because this noble soul was on her way to kneel before the throne of the King of Heaven, himself born among the poor.[8]


## THE SOURCE OF ALL JUSTICE

Who was the first person to truly hunger and thirst for justice? Our Lord Jesus Christ, that blessed man of whom the Beatitudes speak. Born among the desperately poor, he could not even qualify to become a citizen of the empire of his birth. (In fact, as far as we can tell, the only Roman citizen among Jesus' apostles was Saul of Tarsus.)

Citizens who were condemned to death were beheaded, but since Jesus did not enjoy the rights granted to citizens, he died the abysmal death of a slave. Paradoxically, the crucified one is the blessed man.

Christ, who epitomized blessedness, was filled with the eternal light of God, and he leads us to that beacon of divine justice. Woe to us if we do not follow and learn to hunger and thirst for righteousness. Woe if we do not carry the cross of those who suffer. Woe if we shrink back in fear before the spiritual pain of seeing others led astray. Woe if we do not weep and lament when we see those who are dear to us carried away from the kingdom of God.

But if we do hunger and thirst for justice, we must believe that we shall be satisfied, filled, even stuffed. We must believe that by joining our sufferings with those of Christ, by filling up what is lacking in his passion, in some mysterious way we ourselves make a significant contribution to righteousness and to the kingdom of God. We have God's word for it.

*Spirit of fire and truth, Holy Spirit of courage and fortitude, if I am honest with myself I do not really want too much of your gifts. I would like enough courage to make others admire me but I shrink from any courage that would make them disagree with me or despise me. Overcome my weakness and cowardice and feed my soul with your rich and insatiable hunger for righteousness. Satisfy my needs in this earthly life not with fulfillment but with an ever increasing desire to seek your justice and righteousness in the everyday world around me.*

*If I cannot find you among the real needs of real people, then I cannot find you at all and I shall remain forever unsatisfied. Give to your people your gift of courage that we may hunger and thirst insatiably in this world. Then we may surely drink from your everlasting springs in the next. Amen.*

# CHAPTER 6

# The First Beatitude of Illumination: Giving God a Blank Check

*Blessed are the merciful, for they shall obtain mercy.*

*T*wenty-five years ago I sat in a humble, sparse apartment in a rundown tenement on the lower east side of Manhattan. The tiny living room had been transformed into a plain but prayerful chapel. The elderly sister who looked at me was a study in calm contrast. Her face would have intrigued any of the great photographic artists of our time. It showed the effects of age and chronic illness, but it also radiated an inner light and peace which would have captivated any perceptive person. Her name was Sr. Mary Mercy.

Although none of her personal surroundings suggested it, Sr. Mercy was a renowned missionary physician and one of the best known of the Maryknoll Sisters. She had worked for years in the Orient as a physician for the very poor. That part of her life is told in a biography, *Her Name Is Mercy*.[1]

In her old age Sr. Mercy had joined two other Maryknoll sisters, Regina and Eileen, in an effort to bring a contemplative prayer presence to a very poor part of the vast slums of New York City. The intrepid foundress of the Maryknoll Sisters, Mother Mary Joseph Rogers, had established a cloister next to the mother house as a spiritual engine for the missions of this great American community. There the sisters lived humbly and quietly in the tenement. But they had become known to the people of this wildly colorful neighborhood. They attended St. Bridget's Church and were well cared for spiritually by the parish priests, especially Fr. Ed Keehan, who enjoyed his unforeseen role as a chaplain of contemplative nuns.

Now Sr. Mercy was a great realist, as one might expect of a physician who had worked around the world. The twinkle in her eye often let you know that she thought more deeply about things than appeared on the surface of the conversation. At times I'm sure she thought I was off base in some of my youthful enthusiasms, but she was always merciful. It was just that twinkle in her eye that kindly suggested I might be missing some obvious point.

This holy woman's life had a profound impact on my own; I recall one encounter with her that brought me up short and made me realize that I was gliding over deceptively deep waters. Sr. Mercy's conversation was very quiet and plain, like the room we sat in. I noticed some audio tapes on the table—talks given years before by Thomas Merton to the Trappist novices.

"Have you listened to these?" I asked her.

She smiled and said, "I can't listen to them. I can't listen to anything. I can hardly read anything because it's all so complicated. My prayer is very simple, very simple." She saw my incomprehension, smiled broadly, and said, "You see, I am a very simple soul." It is my impression that Sr. Mercy was in contact with—in fact, absorbed into—the light of the merciful Savior whom she had followed faithfully all her life.

## LIGHT ON THE PATH

This Beatitude of mercy illustrates the inner workings of the second stage of the spiritual life: the illuminative way. During the first stage, the soul has been purified through the teachings and grace-led experiences of the Holy Spirit. Gradually, the impulses of sin and selfishness cease to dominate; freedom and inner peace begin to replace drivenness and conflict. Don't panic if you still feel like you have a long way to go before emerging from the dim light of the purgative stage. In his mercy, God gives all of us glimpses of divine radiance. Then, perhaps when we least expect it, we may finally enter into a time of quiet prayer and zeal for the kingdom of God, a stage of the spiritual journey that is characterized by light. By the time I had my eye-opening talk with Sr. Mercy, she had lived long in that divine light, I believe.

Light is an especially potent symbol. How utterly dark this world would be without the illumination that God provides. Imagine descending into the deepest coal mine, surrounded by pitch black. The only way your eyes could penetrate the darkness closing in upon you would be by means of the small lamp attached to your miner's hat.

Or imagine being lost way out in the country on a moonless night. The stars could be glorious, but you would hardly be able to see three feet ahead of you—unless you finally spotted a lighted window in the distance. This single, tiny light would look incredibly beautiful as it beckoned you on.

The drama of the Easter vigil makes powerful use of this symbol of light. A single candle is lit at the back of the dark church, and then its flame is spread to hundreds of candles held throughout the congregation. Those gathered to worship the risen Christ watch the light grow brighter and brighter until it overcomes the darkness and illuminates every corner of the sanctuary. I especially like to watch young children who are unfamiliar with this ritual. Their wondering eyes seem to reflect the glow of the Easter candle.

I think divine illumination operates in our spiritual lives in somewhat the same way as a single candle. God promises to shine his light on our pathway, but usually only a few steps ahead at a time. Although on rare occasions a floodlight may break through our fleshly fog, we tend to complain that we've been given only flashlights—with batteries that seem to go dead right at crucial moments! But we don't necessarily need searchlights or laser beams to make progress on our spiritual journey. God is able to use even the dimmest candlelight to illuminate the path ahead.

During the illuminative way, we can expect to hear God speak more directly to our hearts. For example, when we feel an unexpectedly strong impulse to be merciful, what is really happening? The voice of the Holy Spirit is becoming more inwardly audible—not because the Holy Spirit has finally decided to speak any *louder*, but because all the noise, all the din, all the mundane details that consume our attention are becoming more muted.

Have you ever had an experience—perhaps for an hour or a day, maybe even longer—when you felt closer to God and his mercy? Even if you were struggling with some recurring sin or recovering from a deep disappointment, you could feel God's merciful presence surrounding you in a special way.

At such moments of grace, God was calling you to be merciful as well. If you've ever had such an experience, try to hang onto it. During all the other hours when your ears are filled with the incessant din of responsibilities and distractions, remember what it was like to hear God's voice of mercy.

## "PASS THE BUTTER, PLEASE"

As William Barclay points out, the quality which is ascribed to God most consistently in the Old Testament is mercy, *hesed* in Hebrew. It presents God's mercy as an absolute. Psalm 136 stresses it by repeating the following phrase in each of its twenty-six verses: "... because his mercy endures forever." The Latin translation reads, *"Quoniam in eternum misericordia eius,"* because his mercy is everlasting.[2]

We tend to dwell on divine justice as being everlasting, but God's justice is always tempered by his mercy. Were it not for the mercy of God, you and I would have absolutely no hope of salvation.

Mercy reflects another divine quality: faithfulness. God is faithful in showing us his mercy. He doesn't give up as we do when our efforts to be merciful are thwarted. You know how it goes. You forgive someone a dozen times for some annoying quirk and then you just can't take it anymore. "I've had enough! That's it," you finally blurt out. Or maybe you just say to yourself, "The cup is full. You can't demand anymore of me."

A few of us, at certain grace-filled moments, may imagine that we possess infinite patience. This is an illusion. And if you know some devout, merciful, kind, patient, loving Christian soul, you might want to try the "pass the butter test" to see how infinite that patience really is.

Here's how the "butter test" works. Serve a fluffy baked potato or fresh corn on the cob or homemade rolls for dinner. Instruct everyone at the table (except the one who is to be your test subject) to respond appropriately to all requests from that test subject, except when he or she asks for the butter. Tell them to ignore that particular request, as if they hadn't heard a thing.

Those test subjects who are basking in the advanced stages of the illuminative way usually make it to about the fifth query before they turn the whole table upside down or lunge for the butter in a "boarding house reach." Lesser souls have been known to threaten violence when even the third request goes unanswered!

Mercy characterizes our lives in much the same way as patience: more the exception than the norm. Does God expect *us* to be everlasting in mercy? I suspect not. This Beatitude simply calls us to do a better job of practicing mercy in imitation of the Son of God. You don't have to become a saint overnight. Just make an effort to advance a little bit in being merciful and understanding toward others as well as yourself.

## ARE WE MAKING PROGRESS?

Barclay's commentary on the Beatitudes describes the mercilessness of the ancient world. The pagans practiced infanticide, the killing of small children. Some of the Greek philosophers suggested that children who were physically ill or underdeveloped should be destroyed. These sickly children were put into clay jars and suffocated, or sometimes fed to wild beasts. In some places, including even Jerusalem at times, children were sacrificed to pagan gods. Carthage had the worst reputation. "How merciless, how cruel was the ancient world to children," Barclay says.[3]

Barclay never dreamed that within twenty years after he wrote his commentary, the practice of merciless infanticide would become commonplace in the so-called Christian West. Our society directs this lack of mercy toward the unborn and calls it by a different name: abortion.

I remember listening in horror as a professor from Columbia University Law School seriously suggested that children could be murdered up to four days after birth. He reasoned that this would give the parents a chance to obtain a thorough medical examination for the newborn; then they could better decide if they wanted to keep the baby or not. In his mind, a minor shift from inside the womb to outside the womb offered no serious impediment to the parental "right of choice."

While traveling in Japan many years ago, I visited an ancient Buddhist shrine in Kyoto. As I drew nearer, I noticed a small object sitting in front of one of the austere statues of the

Buddha. A closer look revealed a brand new Raggedy Ann doll. Puzzled, I asked the missionary who was showing me around what the doll meant. My guide explained this Japanese custom: "The doll is a votive offering from the parents of a child who was aborted. It is an offering to Buddha so that the child will have a toy to play with beyond the grave."

At many other shrines in Kyoto, I saw more votive offerings for aborted children: dozens of little cloth pinafores or bibs tied onto the arms of the carved images. At least these Buddhist parents felt some sense of responsibility or remorse. At least they thought that they had done something that needed to be atoned. At least they felt some sense of compassion for the lost child. Our own society sadly lacks even that.

Anyone who visits the concentration camp in Auschwitz will be appalled at the piles of little shoes that belonged to the Jewish children who were massacred under Hitler's regime. Unwanted by the government, these innocent children were deemed defective—and therefore dispensable. The horror of the Nazi extermination of children recalls the crime of Pharaoh, who ordered the death of all Hebrew male babies at the time of Moses; or the crime of King Herod, who sought to kill Jesus by commanding that all boys under the age of two be slaughtered. All these innocents were considered dispensable by ruthless rulers determined to hold onto power at all costs.

Today in our society it is unborn children who are considered dispensable. No matter that these are tiny human creatures with beating hearts and measurable brain waves by the end of the third week of life. Who will be next? Children who suffer from physical defects? Mental patients and the aged? Indeed, even as I write this book, advocates of what is ironically called "mercy killing" are pressing for more and more changes in our laws. Who will speak out for true mercy in these critical days?

## MERCY COSTS

Mercy isn't just some pious, benign feeling. As St. James says so pointedly, it isn't just a matter of words; you can't dismiss a hungry or ill-clothed person with a casual remark like, "Go in peace; be warmed and filled" (Jas 2:16). Mercy costs. It absolutely costs. And you must be prepared to pay the cost.

But mercy does not mean being a fool. New York City is an especially difficult place to practice mercy because all sorts of crooks want to cheat you out of everything. The most merciful thing you can do for those who are trying to cheat you is to not let them succeed. But how can you tell the difference? How can you be sure which of the panhandlers lining the streets of Manhattan seriously need food, and which of them want money to support their drug habit?

Actually, one of the sinister and awful advantages of life in New York is that many of the impoverished look so thoroughly destitute that they can't possibly be acting. Trying to help an obviously needy person requires only a few moments. A brief pause allows us to exchange a kindly word and ask how the person is doing, to make a small contribution, or to buy a little food to ease the physical hunger that constantly plagues the poor. These are acts of mercy. And they cost us something, either in time or in money or both.

What if you suspect that someone might be abusing your charity? Decide once and for all not to let it bother you in the least, and then live by that conclusion. Better to take the chance of being cheated than to neglect mercy. Merciless people never have to worry about being cheated; they just don't help *anybody*. Foolish people, on the other hand, help *everybody!* Those who decide to be merciful in an intelligent way should probably expect about a 12 to 15 percent loss on their investment. This is the amount I figure will inevitably go to charlatans or crooks or people who could be helping themselves a bit more than they are.

I remember a fellow named Scotty Brown, one of the few hobos I ever met who actually gave up his wandering life and got himself back together. This older but still able-bodied man said to me in his Scottish accent, "You know, there has got to be something wrong with every one of us who can't take care of ourselves." I agree wholeheartedly. Something *is* wrong with people who can't take care of themselves. But it may not be their fault. We need to look at those who need help through the eyes of mercy.

I suspect that a great many people would *like* to be merciful but are unsure of how to begin and afraid of being cheated. My advice is: take stock of your limited resources—time, money, mercy—and decide what to do with them. Then just try it! And if you're afraid of being cheated, cheer up. You've already been cheated by lots of other people besides the poor: the federal government, many prominent corporations, most financial institutions, and perhaps even some religious organizations!

Peter Grace, the well-known philanthropist, is the founder of Citizens Against Government Waste. This citizens' group estimates that the federal government wastes billions of dollars every year. Having been cheated regularly and repeatedly by these very respectable people, you've managed to live with it. And you've probably lost much more to the government than you're ever going to lose to somebody who needs mercy. In short, the fear of being cheated is not a legitimate reason to avoid practicing mercy.

Mercy doesn't always mean giving alms. It can also express itself in an act of kindness, a simple word of encouragement, an expression of compassion or forgiveness. Nor is mercy limited to needy strangers: all of your friends and relatives can use all the mercy they can get. (Well, I don't know about all of *your* friends, but all of *my* friends appear to need mercy from time to time—and they all tell me quite regularly that I need plenty of it in return.)

Where can we get all of this mercy for ourselves and for

others? God is our unfailing source. He promises a fresh supply whenever we run low. The letter to the Hebrews assures us, "Let us then with confidence draw near to the throne of grace, that we may receive mercy and find grace to help in time of need" (Heb 4:16).

Mercy calls us to a better life, to a way of living which is more real, more generous, more gentle, and more spiritual than we have ever known. If you want to act like a child of God and attain his mercy, if you want to imitate Christ who was most merciful, then you must practice this quality of mercy in your life and accept the grace to be merciful.

The merciful obtain mercy because they realize how desperately they need it. If mercy opens your mind and heart to the needs of someone else, it infallibly will teach you how much *you* need mercy. But take heart: God promises mercy in abundance to those who need it.


## SOFTLY STRONG

St. Augustine tells us that being merciful activates the gift of counsel. This gift allows us to understand other people's problems and discern with them the right action to take for their spiritual well-being. It enables us to help others find a way out of the most difficult situations, or to help them live with themselves if they're struggling with some serious problem or painful circumstance. This aspect of mercy makes it possible for us to extend a helping hand to someone stuck in a pit of misery, or lost in the deep, dark woods of confusion.

St. Augustine teaches that the Holy Spirit enlightens our minds with the gift of counsel on another person's behalf.[4] I am often astonished at the consoling words which come from my own lips to those in need, while at the same time I am incapable of knowing how to manage my own life. God has designed the human race so that we need one another, and so that we can help each other even when we can't help ourselves. He has created mercy.

I used to know some dear souls who sincerely tried to help the poor. They were so wrapped up in their own little spiritual preoccupations, though, that they made miserable meals for the needy. I worked with them one day and ended up physically ill from the food. They failed to realize that we don't feed the poor the worst. We should give them the best if we really believe they represent Christ, which is what he teaches. The Holy Spirit's gift of counsel helps us to give the best—far better than anything we might be able to do on our own.

In her book, *Blessings That Make Us Be,* Dr. Susan Muto sums up how the gift of counsel operates through mercy: "Mercy and compassion encourage us to see behind the external failings of a person to the infinite value of that person. Mercy opens our minds and hearts to sympathy or the ability to suffer with others; to empathy, the ability to understand objectively and assist others. Mercy breaks down the defenses we have, the need to pretend that we are something that we are not. Mercy helps us to identify with others in their great need or failure."[5]

It was mercy that brought Fr. Damien to share the suffering of the lepers on the island of Molokai. On the dreadful morning when he realized that he had contracted leprosy, it was mercy that put into his mouth the words, "*We* lepers."

In our own lives, it is mercy that allows us to form deep and lasting friendships in this world. If you consistently fail to extend mercy and forgiveness to others, you will never be able to endure anyone long enough to get past a superficial acquaintance. If you want to join a religious community, a parish, a prayer group, or a social club, you had better pray for this Beatitude to be operative in your life. Some of that mercy must be extended to your priests, believe me. We need mercy just like everybody else, and we don't always do such a good job of being merciful to others.

If you want to get married and have children, you had better pray for huge vats full of mercy. You'll need lots of it to keep on forgiving your spouse and your children for their shortcomings. If you are a senior citizen, you will need mercy to understand and accept the ingratitude of those who may have been on the receiving end of your own merciful care for many years.

## THE POWER OF MERCY

Mercy burns up the IOU's of life. It generously forgives debts, even emotional or psychological wounds. Mercy writes a blank check, even to an enemy. Rightly practiced, it never says, "I can forgive anything but *that*."

Pam Moran, who helped me with this book, provides the following account based on the experience of a Dutch Christian woman, Corrie ten Boom. During the Nazi occupation of Holland, this remarkable woman and her family were sent to Auschwitz because they had hidden Jews in their home. There Corrie soon came to hate the sneering guard who mocked their naked bodies whenever they were taken to the showers. His repugnant face was forever seared into her memory.

Corrie watched her sister die in the camp, but she survived and vowed never to return to Germany. Many years later, however, she did return for a speaking engagement. Her first talk centered on the topic of forgiveness: extending the mercy of God to those who have wronged us in some way. To her absolute horror, there, sitting in the audience, was the same guard who had so taunted them at Auschwitz.

This man could not possibly have remembered Corrie as one of his emaciated and shorn prisoners, but she would have recognized him anywhere. Yet on this occasion, he looked decidedly different; his face bore a radiant expression that suggested a dramatic transformation had taken place in his life. Nonetheless, Corrie had no desire to renew their acquaintance.

As it turned out, she had no choice. After her talk, the smiling man approached her and extended his hand. "A fine message, *fräulein*! How good it is to know that, as you say, all our sins are at the bottom of the sea!"[6]

Feeling only intense hatred for this person who had inflicted such pain, Corrie ten Boom heard the Lord tell her to put out her hand. She described what happened:

And so woodenly, mechanically, I thrust my hand into the one stretched out to me. And as I did, an incredible thing took place. The current started in my shoulder, raced down my arm, sprang into our joined hands. And then this healing warmth seemed to flood my whole being, bringing tears to my eyes.

"I forgive you, brother!" I cried. "With all my heart!"[7]

The stored-up hatred of years was melted away in a moment by the warm oil of God's mercy. Could you have endured such horrible abuse and been able to take the hand of your tormentor?

But stop to consider the suffering on the other side. If you had been a twenty-year-old male citizen of Germany in 1940, would you have obeyed orders to machine-gun Jewish mothers, daughters, and babies into a muddy trench grave? Over four decades later, this grim question still haunted the grown children of those who had perpetrated such horrors. Because their fathers had systematically exterminated millions of innocent people, the Germans of the next generation silently carried an enormous burden of guilt and shame.

Many of these men and women did not know what their own fathers had done until after the war. Some were well into their adult years by the time they found out. One woman couldn't sleep without sedatives for decades after learning the horrible truth about her father. A man was able to accept the fact that he even had a father only after working with a support group made up of others with the same history.

By a curse of ancestry, these individuals felt that they themselves were somehow guilty of murder, as if they bore that same evil seed inside their own souls. Coming to see their fathers as separate human beings and to look upon them with mercy and compassion was an extremely difficult journey.

It wasn't until forty-five years after the Holocaust that these tormented Germans were able to break their silence. Ironically, it happened with the help of a Jew, an Israeli psychologist named Dan Bar On. No one else had dared to address the collective or individual guilt of the grown children of Nazi war criminals. Bringing this select group together enabled these anguished men and women to remember, to ask the painful questions, to find some meaning in what had happened, to cleanse themselves of the sins of their fathers.

One member of the group was the son of Martin Bormann, the closest confidant of Adolf Hitler. After the collapse of Germany, young Bormann was taken in by Catholic peasants in Austria. He later decided to convert to Catholicism and become a priest. As an expression of his personal repentance, Bormann served as a missionary in the Congo, where he was tortured in various tribal wars. He learned by painful experience that it was absolutely necessary to forgive, to extend the mercy of God to his enemies. Yet the hardest thing had been to forgive his own father, something which he had to do before he could become a priest.

You and I experience the effects of the sins of our fathers, too, even though they may not have committed such heinous crimes against humanity. Have we been able to admit our own desperate need for the mercy of God? And have we been able to extend that mercy to others, including those who may be nearest and dearest to us? Remember God's promise to give all the mercy we need, if we will approach the throne of grace.

In recent years the attention of many Catholics has been directed to the mercy of God by the revelations of Sister

Faustina. Now beatified, she was a humble Polish lay sister who died as a young woman right before the Second World War.[8] These powerful and profound revelations may have contributed to the publication of the encyclical *Dives in Misericordia* by Pope John Paul II.[9] This great document, *On Divine Mercy,* examines the theological aspects of the mystery of God's mercy for his children. It also makes it clear that Christians must reflect mercy and compassion in their own lives, and work toward a merciful society. The Holy Father brings his message to a close with these stirring words which place the Beatitudes clearly in the center of the spiritual needs of our time.

In the name of Jesus Christ crucified and risen, in the spirit of His messianic mission, enduring in the history of humanity, *we raise our voices and pray* that the Love which is in the Father may once again be revealed at this stage of history, and that, through the work of the Son and Holy Spirit, it may be shown to be present in our modern world and to be more powerful than evil; more powerful than sin and death. We pray for this through the intercession of her who does not cease to proclaim "mercy... from generation to generation," and also through the intercession of those for whom there have been completely fulfilled the words of the Sermon on the Mount: "Blessed are the merciful, for they shall obtain mercy."[10]

*Holy Spirit, Spirit of Counsel, who can teach each of us to surrender our burdens of hurt and anger, help us to be merciful. Instruct us on how to read the hearts of those who need our help, our compassion, our understanding. Give us ears to hear the unspoken cry for mercy that comes from so many we meet every day. Help us to know where and when mercy is required of us as we make our way on the journey toward you. Teach us, above all, the freeing quality of mercy, the grace to be delivered from the prison of our wounded and self-absorbed egos. Grant that we may be merciful and that, at the end of our days, we may obtain that mercy which we so much desire and which we so much need. Amen.*

# CHAPTER 7

# *The Second Beatitude of Illumination: Second-Class Citizens*

*Blessed are the meek, for they shall inherit the earth.*

*F*r. Solanus Casey was a Capuchin priest who spent thirty years caring for the needy and the sick. Unlike most priests, he never received permission to preach or hear confessions. Instead, Fr. Solanus passed those thirty years as a doorkeeper of the Capuchin monastery in Detroit. Nonetheless, his humble service of the poor and his remarkable gifts of healing made him one of the most popular priests of his time. Thousands of people filled Mount Elliot Avenue just to catch a glimpse of his funeral.

Fr. Solanus led an utterly simple life dedicated to doing works of mercy. He never sought any acclaim for himself; in fact, he rejected the notion that he was anything special. After thirty years of pouring himself out for others, he was transferred to St. Felix Friary in Huntington, Indiana, where I happened to be in the novitiate at the time. His superiors wanted Fr. Solanus to enjoy some peace and quiet in his old age, even though he never made such a request for himself.

One day, we were all startled to hear a horn blaring from the parking lot of this remote, rural friary. We novices looked out the window to see a huge tour bus sitting in front of the friary, with a large number of rather rumpled and devout Catholics, mostly elderly women, unboarding after the long trip from Detroit. They were soon scurrying around, in and out of the chapel. They were not leaving without seeing their beloved Fr. Solanus.

This presented a bit of a problem. You see, it was a rule that the secluded friar could receive individual visitors and families, but bus tours were not permitted. The superior, a rather tough German, instructed Fr. Solanus not to go outside. All day long, at three-minute intervals, the bus horn sounded another blast from the parking lot. And hour after hour, Fr. Solanus remained in the chapel with his head bowed in prayer. It would not have crossed his mind to disobey the orders of his superior. Yet you can imagine the deep trial this impasse presented for someone who so loved people.

Finally, at a quarter to five, the superior relented and granted Fr. Solanus the fifteen minutes before evening prayers to go outside and give a blessing to his admirers. I was watching from the window when the old friar came out the door. The entire assembly of fifty or so people fell immediately to their knees. One elderly woman who had been admiring the roses even scurried from the garden on her knees.

In his own humble and self-effacing way, this very simple priest used that fifteen minutes to walk among his kneeling flock. Incredibly, every single person who had journeyed so far had an opportunity to say hello, to hand him a note, to receive a blessing. It seemed like time had stopped. And when the bell rang for the beginning of evening prayers, Fr. Solanus was at his usual place in the choir.

Mercy and meekness had come together on this occasion to lavish love upon those who were hungry. Perhaps we novices were more impressed than anyone else at the humility of this simple priest who now stands on the threshold of beatification. Fr. Solanus obtained mercy and powerfully dispensed God's mercy to many because he himself was merciful and meek.

## MEEKNESS DOESN'T MEAN BEING A *SCHLEP*

Meekness is much harder to define than mercy. In Scripture it refers to a quality that has no exact corresponding term in the English language. Our word "meekness" connotes a kind of weakness. When asked to define meekness, many people would say it means being a sap, a wimp, a doormat who not only allows treadmarks but sometimes even invites them. Meekness is not seen as an admirable quality in our culture, to say the least.

I remember a cartoon depicting a macho guy sporting a large mustache. A bold sign behind the man's desk read: ASSERTIVENESS TRAINING PROGRAM. In front of him sat a puny, sad-sack sort of fellow who was saying, "I just want to be assertive enough so I won't inherit the earth." This poor soul was worried about being able to handle such a huge responsibility! That is not meekness. That is "schlepitude," the quality of being a *schlep*. This fine Yiddish word derives from a German word meaning "someone who plods along."[1]

Scripture refers to Moses as the meekest of men (Nm 12:3). Yet I wouldn't describe Moses as meek when he throws the stone tablets down the side of Mount Sinai at Aaron and all the other Israelites. At least the Moses in Cecil B. De Mille's movie looks anything *but* meek! Michelangelo carved a marble statue of Moses, now among the artistic treasures of Rome's church of St. Peter in Chains. This awesome, heroic figure commands silent admiration rather than scorn.

Our Lord is referred to as meek. In fact, Jesus says of himself: "learn from me; for I am gentle and lowly in heart" (Mt

11:29). But when you read about his kicking the money changers out of the temple, or scathingly rebuking the scribes and Pharisees, you would probably not characterize Jesus as meek.

How does Scripture understand the quality of meekness? According to William Barclay, it means first and foremost accepting the will of God, embracing whatever the Lord sends into our lives so that he can lead us and strengthen us in whatever way he may choose.[2] This humble submission to God's will enables us to find salvation and holiness right where he has placed us, and then to do something with what we have been given. In a sense, meekness means giving God a blank check.

Meekness characterizes those who consider themselves poor—poor in a very real sense. The Hebrew word for the impoverished is *anawim*, those who have little or nothing but God. Those who are meek have relinquished many of their own preferences and claims to importance. They willingly assume the status of second-class citizens in a world greedy for power and wealth.

The Greeks entertained a different notion of meekness. They envisioned a person who was moderate, who did not inflict his or her needs, emotions, and opinions on everyone else. This reticent, middle-of-the-road type of person also corresponds to the oriental idea of meekness. The Japanese, for example, idealize character traits such as expressing deference and avoiding any hint of ostentation—characteristics that don't exactly fit the "ugly American" stereotype.

These Greek and oriental notions of meekness certainly advocate attractive qualities if practiced with genuine humility. But these attributes of moderation and deference aren't necessarily supernatural in origin or in action. Neither do they automatically equate having surrendered one's life and will to God.

The Jewish notion of meekness goes much deeper. It calls for a person to accept God's providence absolutely, however mysterious it may seem, while struggling on to do the best one can. This sort of meekness can stir up conflicts with other people and cause deep anguish in one's relationship with God. We can see this in Psalm 88, for example. My friend Rabbi David Blumenthal, Professor of Judaic Studies at Emory University, has expressed this conflict in his book on the Holocaust, challengingly entitled *Facing the Abusing God*.[3]

In a very thorough examination of the conflict between good and evil, focusing especially on the horrible genocide perpetrated by the Nazis, Blumenthal concludes:

> We cannot forgive God and concentrate on God's goodness. Rather, we will try to accept God—the bad along with the good—and we will speak our lament. We will mourn the bad, and we will regret that things were, and are, not different than they are. This face-to-Face alone will enable us to maintain our integrity, even though it leaves an unreconciled gap between us and God. These steps alone will enable us to have faith in God in a post-holocaust, abuse-sensitive world. Unity and reconciliation are no longer the goal; rather, we seek a dialogue that affirms our difference and our justness, together with our relatedness to God.

Rabbi Blumenthal admits that many Holocaust survivors do not take this position; they are unwilling to judge God and use good and worthy actions to deal with the conflict. He also points out that many serious Christians do not agree with the approach he suggests.[4]

One could conclude that respectful and even filial anger at God is an exclusively Jewish position, one lacking the insight of the New Testament. But this is too facile a conclusion. Most Christians have not experienced anything like a Holocaust. In our century, those who have died (proportionately few, compared with one-third of the Jewish population who perished at the hands of the Nazis) have usually been killed for what they *believed* and not for what they were at birth.

Some Christians, however, may be able to ponder Dr. Blumenthal's reflections in light of their own experiences. I remember a deeply moving conversation with an Armenian bishop who had been born during the genocide of his people. He told me that it was difficult for many of the Christian survivors to forgive God.

What can help us to understand suffering and meekness? One simple way is to look at Jesus on the cross. It is my impression that the Christian spiritual impulse to identify with Christ in his suffering and death—which is seen as a personal act of love for the individual as well as for all who are saved—gives meekness a new meaning and depth. This does not cancel out other forms of meekness, as seen in the lives of the prophets and pre-Christian saints, for example. But the image of the crucified God, who was led like a lamb to the slaughter, must have its effect on the world view of those who make it the focus of their spiritual lives.

With this image in mind I would encourage you to nurture the two obvious aspects of meekness—humbly accepting God's will and practicing moderation in your own needs and demands. Ask yourself these questions as a way to measure meekness in your own life:

1. Are you willing to accept where God has placed you, to be at peace with it, and to do the best you can wherever you are?

2. Are you a person of moderation, one who doesn't do anything to such an excess that you unduly become a cause of discomfort for others?

3. Are you willing in imitation of Christ to surrender even moderation in favor of self-denial when you face the demands of justice or of Christian charity?

As you make these two qualities your aim—especially the acceptance of God's will—you will find yourself advancing in the spiritual life. You will experience a deepening inner composure that helps you to pray and to do the will of God. And you will gradually experience more of God's light illuminating the pathway of your own spiritual journey.

## MEEKNESS AND FIDELITY

We will make even further progress in holding heaven in our hands if our meekness is strengthened by the spiritual gift of fidelity or piety. Through the operation of this gift, the Holy Spirit enables us to put everything in life into proper perspective with respect to life after death, to eternal life, and to the spiritual life both now and in the hereafter.

The name of this spiritual gift is a bit confusing. The word "piety" derives from the Latin word *pietas*. This does not mean "religious devotion," as it does in modern English. When we say that someone is pious, we mean devout. But the Latin meaning of piety connotes loyalty and fidelity. It means being loyal despite all obstacles and untoward events—even apparent rejection.

In writing of the meek who possess the land, St. Augustine describes meekness as a quality that stands for "something solid, the stability of an undying inheritance when the soul, in a state of well-being, rests as if in its natural environment as a body does on the earth."[5] He goes on to identify the meek as those who yield before outbursts of wickedness, who do not resist evil, but overcome evil with good.

In an especially insightful text, Augustine writes of the relationship of the gift of piety or fidelity to meekness by describing the meek person in these terms: "He who seeks a godly or pious frame of mind honors Holy Scripture and does not find fault with what as yet he does not understand. Therefore he does not oppose it, which is what it is to be meek."[6]

Meekness taught the saints to find God where they were. Meekness permitted many of the victims of the Holocaust not to lose hope in the midst of horror. Meekness helps us to believe that God can bring us into a place of light when we feel surrounded by darkness or filled with despair. Meekness helps us to accept things about ourselves that we don't like, and to believe that we may overcome them over the course of time with the help of God's grace.

Meekness also means being willing to listen to the pastoral office of the Church, even when we disagree—or *especially* when we disagree. Meekness helps us to do what we're supposed to do when we can't make any sense out of it ourselves. Out of genuine meekness, we may willingly take on a burden that other people would reject. If so, we will be rewarded by God.

With hindsight, many people cannot understand the failure of so many Jews and Christians to mount any resistance to the terror unleashed by Hitler. The simple fact is that many devout people were absolutely trapped by evil. They were capable of fidelity but not of resistance. Those who were more resourceful, and perhaps even more courageous, took chances and escaped or helped others escape. I hope I would have had the grace to be one of them.

But others were simply trapped. Those who hid Jews or helped them escape risked an agonizing fate in the concentration camps. Those caught by the Gestapo who showed any defiance were killed on the spot.

Millions faced death with a certain dignity and self-possession that others may have perceived as weakness. I read of one old Jewish man in Belarus who, knowing the fate that would befall his protectors if he were discovered, simply walked out into the street when the SS guards swarmed through the village, shouting, "Jews come out, come out and face death." While some may perceive this behavior to reflect a kind of weakness, I would suggest a different explanation: perhaps these victims of Nazi brutality were actually practicing the heroic virtue of meekness. They had no place to go, and so they stood there and took the cruel treatment God had permitted to come into their lives.

By the way, I do not deny that God is mysterious, but I do not think in any way that he caused these atrocities. Still, the question is a hard one. The forces of evil eventually perished in a terrible judgment, but we still wonder: Why did God not spring the trap of those snared by this evil before millions had suffered torture or death? The Lord did not bend the heavens and come down to rescue the innocent, just as he did not come down to free Jesus from the torment of the cross. Meekness does not answer the speculative question—but it does tell us, practically, what to do.

Sometimes the stability of meekness is what makes it possible for an ordinary person to face inescapable doom with dignity and faith. Many a martyr has done simply that and in death has defeated his enemies. But this is meekness in the worst of all possible circumstances. Even in the more commonplace challenges of life, meekness is a powerful means of accomplishing something worthwhile, of receiving more of God's light and taking that next step in our spiritual journey. Meekness gives an alcoholic the strength to get up at an Alcoholics Anonymous meeting and say for the first time, "My name is Joe. I am an alcoholic." That is exactly what it means to be meek. The meek don't seek excuses for what they may have done wrong. Rather than spending a lot of time defending what was ill advised or sinful, the meek pursue opportunities to change for the better.

Sometimes meekness is best reflected in clinging faithfully to whatever we *do* know rather than fretting so much about what we *don't*. The Swedish Nobel Prize winner Par Lagerkvist wrote a compelling novel, *The Sybil*, which focuses on the servant in an ancient pagan temple. This man realizes that the image he worships is a long way from God, but he doesn't know any other way to reach him. In fact, he actually disapproves of many of the temple's pagan practices—just as you might feel serious qualms about something you see going on in the Church from time to time. But it is all this sacristan knows about how to find God, and so he sticks with it. He is a meek man and the reader suspects he will be blessed by God. Is he a symbol of those who "will come from east and west... and sit at table in the kingdom of God" (Lk 13:29)?

Meekness makes the crucial difference in enabling us both to be faithful to whatever we do know—and pliable to the workings of the Holy Spirit who leads us to what we *don't* know.

## "I WILL NOT SERVE!"

Of all the Beatitudes we have discussed so far, I think this one may be the most necessary to our spiritual growth. A lack of meekness brings out the worst in us: the most childish, egocentric, self-centered voice that either whines incessantly or else shouts emphatically, "I will not serve!"

Pride, identified as the greatest enemy of our souls by Scripture and by saints like Augustine and Francis, can be undone by the power of meekness. Meekness seems to mark the cutting edge between angels and devils. Lucifer's proud refusal to serve lost him the possession of heaven, while Michael's willingness to obey brought him eternal bliss (Rv 12:7ff). The New Testament names these mysterious figures, so distant from our own experience, to warn us of the necessity of meekness and fidelity if we wish to inherit the kingdom of heaven.

God will not coerce a human being who says, "I will not serve." But on the other hand, refusing to serve does not change the will of God any more than jumping out of a window would change the law of gravity. A disagreement between you and God inevitably demonstrates who holds the greater power. You won't break the will of God; you will simply break your bones against his will. The meek person does not take that leap of pride and provoke a confrontation.

It's no secret that I look with a jaundiced eye on a lot of what goes on in our present world. As I mentioned earlier, I'm not generally very impressed by the twentieth century. Any century during which at least a hundred million people have been killed in wars can't be such a great historical era. But in the midst of everything, I am filled with hope, joy, and thanksgiving because of the significant number of people I see all around me who are growing in holiness and practicing the Beatitude of meekness. If the devil is going to be defeated in our time, he will be defeated first and foremost by the meek.

I see many people struggling against tremendous odds with the collapse of family life, with the epidemic of infidelity that has attacked marriage. I see parents struggling against the destructiveness of our pagan culture that beats down upon their children. They don't give up following Christ, but keep on trying to love in the best way they can.

I see many of the younger generation resisting the forces of hell that have been unleashed against them in the media and anticulture. I see many adults in all walks of life giving up the pleasures of sin to be molded by God. I see members of religious communities being loyal and faithful in the face of serious disappointment, such as the loss of vocations or even the certain end of their particular order. I see many people struggling with homosexual tendencies and other kinds of sexual difficulties that they never asked for but must overcome in their quest to follow the gospel.

As a priest, I hear a lot of confessions. People come with horrendous spiritual and moral dilemmas. They say, "Father, I am a sinner. I've got a terrible problem." It's too bad they have this difficulty, but at least they're admitting it. I am glad and rejoice that at least they are meek. Meekness is a great virtue, the beginning point of the other virtues, I believe. I am not so concerned whether people struggle successfully, but I am very impressed when they battle on with meekness.

Catholics demonstrate this virtue when they come and confess their sins. They humbly admit their neediness before the one who created them. God has already forgiven billions of sins and he will certainly forgive billions more. Why? Because *his mercy endures forever.* But there is one sin that God cannot forgive: the sin that is not repented. Meekness allows us to repent and then God can pour out his mercy upon us.

## WHAT DOES IT MEAN TO INHERIT THE EARTH?

Scripture says that the meek will inherit the earth. Such a promise strikes our ears as rather grandiose, like hyperbole or grand overstatement. It obviously does not mean the earth in which we live; it means the heavenly world. Our reward for meekness involves spiritual realms, blessings that will last forever.

However, the meek do in a strange way inherit a sizable portion of this world. Do you know how? The meek survive. Did anybody ever say to you, "Oh, you're a survivor"? That means you have a basic kind of meekness. No matter what happens, no matter how terrible things turn out to be, no matter what disasters befall you, you keep trying to find the will of God in those circumstances and keep going.

If you're a believer who is struggling to make progress in the spiritual life, you already have a kind of meekness or you wouldn't still be trying. No matter what the odds, God will give you the grace to fight another battle, until the day is finished and the race is run.

Those who are not meek often die of rage or frightful disappointment or sheer desperation. Because they can't tolerate things as they are, they may violate the notion of meekness every way they turn. Unwilling to find the hand of God leading them through the worst of situations, they may become inordinate in their anger. My friend Msgr. Arthur Rojek, who survived four and a half years in Auschwitz and Dachau, once told me that many prisoners who did not survive died of sheer rage.

Those who die of rage do not have the meekness of Christ, who walked through this earth as the meekest of men even though he was also God. Jesus saw his life's work destroyed on Thursday night but resolutely went on to Calvary. Meek were the last words Jesus spoke from the cross: "Father, forgive them for they know not what they do.... Father, into your hands I commend my spirit." Here we find meekness in its purest form: the meekness of God.


## THE MEEK SHALL CHANGE THE WORLD

In whatever small and homely ways God may lead the meek, he often leads them to do a good in a place where no one else will or can do that particular good. I've chosen one man to illustrate this principle, someone who had a profound effect on the history of the world and of the Church. He is an unknown man whose influence is still being felt long after his death.

This man appeared on the scene during an especially difficult time in his native land. By means of a brutal military occupation, the Nazi forces were doing everything possible to obliterate all culture and religion in Poland. In some parts of the country, children were not allowed to attend school or any religious services. They were manipulated to become mindless slaves of the state, pawns of the government.

Cardinal Glemp, the Archbishop of Warsaw, has recounted his own childhood memories from those grim years. As a boy he went to Mass five times in five years. He had no education at all apart from what his mother gave him at home (against the express orders of the state).

In such a bleak time, one man decided to start a discussion group on the writings of the Fathers of the Church and the mystics. He wasn't a theologian or a priest or a religious. He was a tailor by trade, a man named Jan Tyranowski who earned his living by sewing clothes and making suits.[7] He actually had a limited formal education, but he could read the great classics and he became an expert on the writings of St. John of the Cross.

Realizing the people's need for culture, Tyranowski introduced young people to a theater group where the actors and audience were all one and the same. They met in utter secrecy under cover of darkness because the Nazis had absolutely forbidden public assemblies. Apart from some limited worship services, the Polish people were allowed to congregate only when they shared meals.

Even though it was an extremely dangerous venture, Tyranowski repeatedly risked his life by recruiting people to study and learn the art of meditation. One day the tailor walked up to a young man in the back of a church and introduced himself. Tyranowski said, "I've noticed you here at church a few times. Would you like to come to our discussion group?"

The young man was frightened, and rightly so. This stranger could be a Nazi spy or a member of the Gestapo, and so he treated Tyranowski's invitation with apparent indifference. But the hero of our story would not give up. Since they lived in the same neighborhood, the tailor insisted on walking home with his potential recruit. Finally, because he had been importuned, the young man agreed to go. After all, he had a strong interest in the theater, as well as in the mystics.

As he studied, his life began to change. Under the threat of death from the Nazis, this young man named Karol went on to study for the priesthood. He eventually became Pope John Paul II. His vocation came because an apparently very ordinary man, a tailor, was willing to discover in that dreadful situation an opportunity to do something good. Rather than despair, the tailor had the courage to create change. Tyranowski offered light and illuminated the way for this young man who had so much potential.

Some Poles risked their lives through armed resistance. But blowing up trains and bridges wasn't Tyranowski's style. This meek tailor didn't believe in violence. Rather he taught people; he opened their minds; he planted seeds in the midst of a harsh winter. He continued doing good when there was absolutely no hope in sight.

Tyranowski didn't waste his energy complaining to God because a brutal injustice had fallen upon his homeland. He didn't pine away with fear and trembling. This meek man ran a discussion group—a very little item on the stage of world events. And through it, he changed the history of the Church and the world.

The election of a Polish pope, especially a man of such intelligence and personal strength, has opened the door for momentous world reform. Pope John Paul II has in all meekness confronted the fiercest totalitarian governments and insisted that their citizens be granted freedom and basic human rights. Now that the Iron Curtain has finally been torn down, the pope continues to challenge the forces of evil in the world at every turn.

Without guns, without force, with no strength except that which derives from God's grace, Pope John Paul II has shaped world history. Why? Because there was once a tailor who was a meek man, who found God's will right where he was. Tyranowski died when Karol Wojtyla was doing his graduate studies in Rome.[8] He never had the slightest notion that his simple invitation would so dramatically affect the history of the world.

What if we were able to meet Tyranowski and credit him with influencing John Paul II to become a priest? I believe the tailor would laugh or shrug his shoulders and say, "Nobody becomes a priest unless God calls him. I didn't give out vocations; I just ran a discussion group." What if we could point out to him that this scholarly young man wrote his doctoral dissertation on St. John of the Cross because of the discussion group? Since Tyranowski was a meek man, I believe he would again shrug his shoulders and say, "Oh, Karol would have heard of St. John of the Cross someplace else."

In our daily lives, in our struggles, in our failures, in our good deeds, and even in repenting for our frequent sins, may God give us mercy and meekness by the grace of the Holy Spirit. And may he grant us the gift of fidelity to know that even though no one may recognize what we do, though we may live and die in utter obscurity, if we are meek we shall indeed inherit the earth and the heavens.

～

*Come, Holy Spirit, gentle, silent Spirit of God, and teach us to be meek and humble of heart. Help us to learn from Jesus the virtue that accompanied him when he was alone on the cross. All appeared to have been lost, but Jesus was still clothed with meekness. Fidelity to the Father's will brought him to the cross, and all around him was filled with signs of meekness. Before the fiery flash of the resurrection there was the soft light of meekness to encourage the suffering, to strengthen the penitent, to beckon the sinner.*

*Help us to be faithful in trials, to be steadfast in difficulties, even brave in the face of sickness and death. Then we shall make ourselves meek beneath the mighty hand of God. But, O Holy Spirit, give us also wisdom that we may resist evil as best we can, that meekness may never be negligence or cowardice. Give us the meekness of the martyrs who fought the good fight and who went on in the face of all that evil could do, confident that a kingdom lay before them. Amen.*

# CHAPTER 8

# The Third Beatitude of Illumination: Doing the Work of God

*Blessed are the peacemakers, for they shall be called the sons of God.*

*H*ave you ever met people who seem imperturbable, no matter what anybody else does, no matter what injustices or ingratitude come their way? And they seem to achieve this peace effortlessly, without the virtuous restraint that indicates when someone is really *trying* to be patient. Such models of serenity are few and far between.

And then you look at yourself. If you've been struggling for a long time with repentance and prayer, sooner or later you are bound to become terribly rattled, upset, disappointed, annoyed, or confused. Yet down in the depths of your soul, a tiny pocket of peace remains, a small cleft in the rocks where there is calm, no matter how bad the day becomes.

Even when you momentarily lose track of this deep, inner

stronghold, it usually resurfaces fairly soon. I'm not speaking about a fleeting emotion like happiness or even inner joy. I mean a safe harbor from the storms of everyday life, a shelter that allows you to survive. This peace is more than just a conviction; it is a discovery.

A friend once sent me a snapshot taken four decades ago when we were in the novitiate together. The photo shows me as a seventeen-year-old sitting on a park bench talking to my father. When I first looked at it, I immediately noticed how incredibly I had aged since then! Then I was struck by how peaceful and contented I looked in the photo. I remember asking myself, "How in the world did this boy ever survive all these years? He looks so terribly vulnerable."

Survival at best—that has literally been my experience. But I have survived the swirling tides of life because I discovered a little harbor inside my soul—a haven that I didn't build, a refuge that I didn't set apart from the winds of life. Sometimes, in the midst of storms, I couldn't find this sanctuary, but I knew it was there anyway.

Because he is the God of peace, the Father provides this inner haven for each of us, a shelter that allows us to survive during difficult times, a place where we can receive the light of grace. If we are trying desperately to hold onto him, God will allow us to find this precious place of peace. He will hold out his hand.


PEACE, PEACE, AND THERE IS NO PEACE

We hear a lot about peace these days, perhaps because the human race has grown so weary of war. With the winding down of the cold war, many people envisioned a more tranquil world. They thought that the end of the Soviet challenge meant peace over the next horizon. Instead, the shattered remnants of the Communist empire now face overwhelming challenges in trying to establish peace and order.

Tension and violent conflict continue to wreak havoc in many nations. Ethnic and religious disputes that have smoldered for centuries have blazed into widespread death and destruction in Europe, Africa, and the Middle East, in places as different as Bosnia, Somalia, and the Holy Land. Tribal groups and whole nations seem to disintegrate before our very eyes. Years from now, these particular conflicts may be old news, but others will have certainly taken their place.

Every once in a while we human beings become fed up with war. With some dreamy look in our eyes, we voice our heartfelt hope that the violence lurking in the human heart has finally expressed itself to the ultimate absurdity. We boldly proclaim that we are now on the threshold of lasting world peace.

In 1945, as in 1918, many believed that there would be no more wars. Now, despite the most concerted diplomatic efforts, we find ourselves as far from world peace as we were then. The United Nations resolutely warns its unruly members against ignoring the provisions of its charter. Unless such defiance of world order is reversed, we may be plunged into a third world war that will make the last one look tame.

The violence in our own cities brings the problem much closer to home. The cultural melting pot called America brews ongoing racial and ethnic conflict. While the government and legal system work overtime to sort out the countless inconsistencies and inequalities, those who suffer injustice often resort to more direct methods of achieving the American dream. Now and then these outbreaks of violence escalate to warlike dimensions. The Los Angeles riots of 1992, for example, were billed in some news magazines as the most destructive domestic clash since the Civil War.

Some of us have to function in the middle of this insanity every day. Various chores often take me from our friary in the noisy Bronx or from the quiet of Trinity Retreat to midtown Manhattan and other sections of New York City. Mugging and murder are commonplace. Children quickly learn to duck whenever they hear gunfire. All have learned to live with a certain amount of fear.

Police struggle to maintain some sense of law and order, but this is hardly peace. Even a squad of professional commandos would be hard pressed to keep crime in check in this vast metropolis. On my way to speak at a recent conference on the topic of peace, I had to walk right through a scene of deep and angry conflict in the shadow of a great university. I thought, *How strange it is to be speaking of peace in the middle of this great city where there is such an absence of peace.*

Yet Jesus tells us that we are to be peacemakers. While this saying may roll off the tongue like a well-oiled pearl of wisdom, we must never take these words lightly. This most popular of the Beatitudes contains much more than meets the eye. It calls us not to experience or to enjoy peace, but to *make* it happen.


## SOLDIERS FOR PEACE

Some years ago I was invited to speak at the baccalaureate Mass at West Point military academy. It was a rather odd invitation, I thought, because I had always involved myself in activities related to peace. But then I had also been annoyed by those peace enthusiasts who so readily heap blame upon soldiers. (For a long time I've distanced myself from people who loudly proclaim the cause of peace with great self-righteousness. Oddly enough, they tend to be among the angriest people I've ever met.) I decided to go to West Point.

More than those in any other walk of life, military personnel shoulder a unique responsibility for peace. Soldier-saints like St. Martin of Tours and St. Joan of Arc responded to this obligation in exemplary ways. During his years as a soldier, Martin befriended a destitute victim of war and thus became the medieval patron saint of charity. Joan demonstrated mercy and compassion even for her enemies and tried to save them. She prayed fervently before and after military engagements for the souls of all who would die in battle.

In my West Point sermon, I preached to the graduates mostly about their responsibility to be soldiers of peace, whether in periods of peace or in times of war. I thought my words might make some of the powers that be uncomfortable. Quite the contrary. The superintendent of the academy seemed delighted with my theme. He even requested a copy of my talk to distribute to the cadets. Even though he himself was not a Catholic, this man said to me, "Father, the message of peace you gave here today is the most important thing that we could communicate to these potential officers." It was not said as a trite remark. I believe he meant it very sincerely.

Those who urge nonviolence sometimes protest by picking on the military. I can't think of anything more nonsensical. Do firefighters want fires or police want crime? Of course soldiers don't want war! Perhaps in earlier times war was somewhat exalted as "the glorious battle." At this stage of history, however, televised, on-the-spot reports from the scenes of battle have smashed any such illusions. They are powerful, visual reminders that war is always and everywhere an iniquitous calamity, one which falls most heavily upon those who must fight on the front lines, and the civilians who are tragically caught in the middle.

Archbishop John Ryan, the former archbishop of the Archdiocese of the Military Services, once stated that no Christian can be exempted from the responsibility of working for peace. The archbishop offered three ways in which we might carry out this Christian obligation. He first mentioned conscientious objection as a valid way to protest against war. In fact, Franz Jagersdauter, a devout Austrian church sexton who was beheaded by the Nazi government for conscientiously objecting to military service, has been proposed for beatification.

The second way to work for peace involves public protest. Archbishop Ryan defended such activities as a legitimate means of bringing this issue before government leaders. The third way is serving in the armed forces—providing the government is sincerely working for justice, human rights, and world peace. The archbishop also stressed that soldiers must never forget that their primary responsibility is to be peacemakers.

I don't think the idea of soldiers for peace is silly or far-fetched. If you ever find yourself in the middle of an armed conflict facing members of the opposing army, I hope they are soldiers of peace. I hope they feel responsible for protecting your rights as a human being, for taking prisoners rather than killing them, for showing justice and compassion in the face of the calamity of war. If you are a parent, you would certainly utter this same prayer for your son or daughter who had to go off to war. And you can rest assured that people from every other country feel precisely the same way. Blessed be the soldiers for peace.

Many of you may not be able to work for peace in any of these three ways. You may not be the demonstrating type. You may be too old to sign up for the military or to be a conscientious objector. Threatening to turn in your draft card from the Korean War would elicit only laughter.

Then what *can* you do? You start in your own backyard. You pursue peace with your family, friends, fellow parishioners, and co-workers. Having begun your campaign for harmony at home, you can then extend your efforts on a broader scale.

For instance, Americans live in a country that has one of the most powerful militaries in the world. We who make up the electorate cannot exonerate ourselves from the responsibility of pursuing peace. Whatever political party you support, you need to bring appropriate and effective pressure to bear upon your state and federal representatives to work for peace. Worthwhile goals include the reduction of armaments and the aggressive pursuit of justice and peace on the international scene.

It is worth noting that while sane soldiers want peace (for reasons of personal survival if nothing else) those who produce weapons may want war. The vast industrial complex known as the war industry is a mindless financial monster which gobbles up money to make things we hope we never need, like nuclear weapons. This monster, often directed by personally decent and law-abiding folk, has a vast influence over our national policy, an influence fed by fear. It is a very sobering thought to realize that many of the petty but bloody wars of recent years have been fought with weapons of destruction provided to both sides by American taxpayers who were unaware of what they were supporting. It is humiliating and troubling to realize that many missionaries, local clergy, and devout and innocent laity in other countries were murdered in recent years with weapons paid for and produced by the United States, by assassins trained by American personnel who were paid with your tax money. Archbishop Oscar Romero of El Salvador was one of these victims.

If you come from some little country like Liechtenstein or Tobago, you will probably not be asked on the day of judgment what you did to encourage your homeland to pursue peace. But if you come from the United States with its immense military power, I suspect such a question will be quite relevant. A sizable portion of every dollar you earn goes into the manufacture of weapons and the sustaining of the military establishment. You must search your own conscience as to what you could be doing to promote non-violent means for resolving conflict.

## TOWARD THE FULLNESS OF PEACE

Let's look beneath the surface meaning of this Beatitude. William Barclay clarifies what Jesus is saying here: "How full of bliss are those who seek peace or those who make peaceful relationships, for they do the work of God."[1] Although a bit awkward, this alternative translation gives the word "peacemaker" new depth. Peacemakers do not only bring conflict to an end; they also work toward deep and long-lasting reconciliation.

The word "peace," *eirene* in Greek, appears in every book of the New Testament. Christ often used the common Hebrew word *shalom* as a greeting or when speaking of peace. The Jews of old loved this word, meant to convey the prayer, "the Lord give you his peace" or "peace be with you." According to the Jewish Scriptures, peace meant not only the absence of conflict with the rest of the world but, even more importantly, a healthy relationship with God and with family and friends.

Judaism also linked justice and peace. The Jews knew what it was to be enslaved. Having lived in fear under the power of Egyptian slavemasters, they knew that tranquility alone was not enough. True peace required the absence of conflict, *plus* justice and good relationships with those who were important in their lives. They needed the experience of having their rights fulfilled.

The Greeks, on the other hand, didn't espouse quite the same notion of peace, perhaps because they had never been enslaved. They envisioned a controlled state with an absence of conflict, and where those who didn't behave themselves quickly received their just desserts. The ancient Greeks would have settled for less than the Jews. As a democratic nation, they desired a simple absence of conflict; this allowed them ample opportunity to develop and grow. The Jews didn't want just the absence of conflict; they wanted justice and righteousness as well.

When we look at these two notions of peace—both of which are reflected in sacred Scripture—we realize that many people today cannot imagine what peace might be like, either here on earth or in the hereafter. Ask people whose spiritual development and insight have been stunted to describe their image of an eternal life of peace and bliss. You will probably get a description of the "happy hunting ground."

I know one poor fellow who spent all of his life at a bar. When the time finally came to bury him, he wasn't actively involved in any religion—or in anything but his alcoholic recreation. In this man's grand finale, his bar buddies paraded up to the local graveyard to bury the sclerotic corpse. One of the more eloquent mourners had sobered up enough for the occasion to say a few words of farewell: "Well, I really believe Jimmy is now at the everlasting cocktail party."

I don't think I would be comforted to know that such an epitaph were going to be spoken over my casket. Unfortunately, though, I'm afraid this silly statement reflects the world's most common vision of a peaceful hereafter. Secular magazines like *The New Yorker* routinely carry jokes or cartoons depicting heaven and hell. Winged angels flit around on fluffy clouds; little red devils strut around in a fiery furnace.

One way to develop a clearer picture of peace is to imagine its opposite: chaos. In the majestic painting that adorns the Sistine Chapel, Michelangelo attempted to depict the Last Judgment. He contrasted the peace of the heavenly Jerusalem above with the chaotic vision of hell and the river Styx below. In order to meaningfully portray heaven, Michelangelo found he also had to portray hell.

I remember a play named *Green Pastures*, in which God the Father is depicted as an old reverend down in the deep South. He's running heaven like it was a small, black Baptist church, and meanwhile trying to get things organized down on earth with great good humor. I find that a lovely vision of peace.

In contrast, Jean-Paul Sartre presents an awful vision of hell in his play *No Exit*. He brings us into a hotel room where three angry, narcissistic strangers are verbally clawing at each other for all eternity. Try to picture yourself in the middle of such unyielding agony. We catch a glimpse of purgatory in Eugene O'Neill's play, *Long Day's Journey into Night*. A despondent woman's descent into narcotic addiction and the struggles of her family make us wish desperately that she could be finished with her pain.

Music offers similar contrasts. Engraved on the tomb of Sir Henry Purcell is a tribute saying that this composer had to die and go to heaven to hear any music more sublime than his own. The music of Bach and Handel strike my ear the same way. In stark contrast to the glory of *The Messiah* blare the chaotic tones of *The Carmina Burana*, profane songs of the Middle Ages, which have been set to discordant and dissonant music. And what could sound more like the music of hell than the acid rock constantly consumed by some of today's teenagers, complete with diabolical words and hellish sounds? When we juxtapose opposites such as these, we begin to develop a clearer picture of peace.

The prophet Isaiah paints a vivid picture of the peaceful kingdom. He speaks of a land where milk and honey flow freely, where the child plays with the asp and the viper, where the lion lies down with the ox and the lamb. In the peaceable kingdom described in the Book of Revelation, trees bear fruit twelve times a year. As these images show us, peace is not only the absence of evil and chaos, but also the presence of good and tranquility. Although we may have dabbled around the edges of peace for brief moments now and then, the perfect peace these images portray can never be found in this world.

## "LET IT BEGIN WITH ME"

If we want to live up to the challenges of this Beatitude, where do we begin? Well, everyone knows that you always begin with yourself! "Let there be peace on earth and let it begin with me," as the hymn goes. I don't know about you, but when I look inside my own heart, I'm not so sure that peace will ever come to anybody else if it depends on me.

An honest and sincere examination of myself reveals at least a desire for peace. I see that little harbor of tranquility deep inside. I also see whirlpools of rage and other nasty sentiments that cause war within me. I hear all of those terrible relics of original sin—pride, covetousness, lust, anger, gluttony, envy, and sloth—screaming out their vile messages inside my mind.

Although the particular notes may vary from one individual to another, the same chorus of horror resides inside every one of us. War begins in the human heart. It begins with one person making a fearful, warlike decision; with one will setting itself against another. Well aware of this, our Lord Jesus Christ instructed his disciples to use peace as a sort of thermometer of a person's spiritual condition:

> Whatever town or village you enter, find out who in it is worthy, and stay there until you leave. As you enter the house, greet it. If the house is worthy, let your peace come upon it; but if it is not worthy, let your peace return to you. If any one will not welcome you or listen to your words, shake off the dust from your feet as you leave that house or town. Truly I tell you, it will be more tolerable for the land of Sodom and Gomorrah on the Day of Judgment than for that town.
>
> See, I am sending you out like sheep into the midst of wolves; so be wise as serpents and innocent as doves.
>
> **Matthew 10:11-16**

Just as war begins with one person at a time, so does peace. For the Christian, that peace is rooted in obeying the will of God as manifested through the law of Christ. In his book on the Beatitudes, Barclay rightly says that the acceptance of Christ is the beginning of peace.[2] This has been the burden of every papal Christmas message since the 1930s.

We must accept the law of Christ as it is passed on by the Church if we are to have peace within ourselves. Just as there can be no peace in the world without justice, there can be no peace within an individual without the honest pursuit of righteousness. And we will find it impossible to discover the Holy Spirit and his law in our hearts if we do not at least accept the tangible guidance of the Church's teaching that delivers us from our own subjectivism. While it is certainly true that the clergy of any time or place may miss the message of peace, our failure does not diminish the peacemaking message of the gospel. It only proves the universality of the need for constant repentance.

How do we begin to give peace to others? Dr. Susan Muto describes this task as involving a strange blend of restlessness and peacefulness. Once we set out to bring peace to the world, we will inevitably find ourselves at odds with something or someone. The world of nature often opposes us through earthquakes, disease, storms, and famine. The world of human relationships presents us with obstacles like discord, fighting, anger, fury, rage, and war.

## A MEMORIAL TO THE CRAZINESS OF WAR

One time when I was on my way to the foreign missions, I was stranded for a day (courtesy of the airlines) in the grand city of Honolulu (not a bad place to be stranded, I must admit). A good friend of mine, Brother Terence of the Marists, was working there at the Father Damien High School that summer. He offered to show me around. He drove me up to a gigantic military cemetery nestled in the crater of an inactive volcano that looms above the city of Honolulu. Thousands of soldiers are buried there, including some Japanese military personnel.

Huge arches surrounding the cemetery create a cloistered wall, decorated with mosaic maps of the principal battles of the Second World War in the Pacific. The names rang out like a litany of fear, bringing back memories of my childhood: Tarawa, Guadalcanal, Corregidor, the Coral Sea. I remembered listening to the news about the fall of Corregidor, a place that sounded so far away but that suddenly assumed a bloody importance to many people in America. From that day on, the mere mention of this heretofore unknown island would bring fresh pangs of sorrow to the parents and wives and children of those who died at Corregidor.

As we were walking away from the war memorial, I noticed a statement engraved at the beginning of the maps: WAR, AFTER ALL, IS A SPIRITUAL PROBLEM. A spiritual problem indeed, one which boils down to one person at a time. The warlike spirit exists in the soul of a single person. And when enough people share the same spiritual problem, you soon have a war.

On another occasion I visited the Japanese war memorial in Okinawa. Forty thousand Japanese naval and military personnel had died there by the end of the war. With gentle music playing in the background, extremely polite volunteer tour guides ushered us around—openly weeping as they did so. I thought to myself, *Why, these nice people were our enemies and I was their enemy. Fifty years ago we were mortal foes. How crazy!*

How absolutely, positively mad war is. How can we explain it? The only answer: war is ultimately a spiritual problem.

Dr. Victor Frankl, the renowned Austrian psychiatrist who was imprisoned in Nazi concentration camps because he was Jewish, wrote a remarkable book entitled *The Doctor and the Soul*. In it he examines the spiritual aspects of psychological injustice. Frankl saw violence as the direct consequent of denying the spiritual component of human nature. External violence originates in the experience of internal warfare. Human beings without a meaning beyond the physical will be angry, furious, and jealous. They will first be in conflict with themselves and then they will push those around them into war. Frankl saw this happening in Germany. "The gas chambers of

Auschwitz were the ultimate consequence of the theory that man is nothing but the product of heredity and environment or, as the Nazis like to say, 'of blood and soil.'"[3]

## PEACEMAKING CHILDREN OF GOD

At least six times in the New Testament, the Lord is called the "God of peace." Jesus Christ, the Son of God who carries out the peacemaking work of his Father, is called the "Prince of Peace." Despite this clear connection, even Christians find peacemaking difficult, and precious few people appreciate it. Yet those who walk in the footsteps of the peaceful Christ are promised an incredible reward: to be called the children of God.

This means more than simply being legally adopted. A child of God means someone who does the work of God. The makers of peace are called not only heirs of God but active members of the divine family, offspring who do the same work as their Father.

How do you continue to make peace in this world rather than sow discontent? Dr. Muto offers an eloquent answer:

Jesus' love and peace will enlarge our hearts if we remain attuned to the movement of the Spirit, to the aspirations and inspirations that guide our formative journey. Peace is a sign that we are living in Christ's presence, a deep tranquility that remains there even in the midst of tension. We can trust that we are walking with Christ and following his direction if there is no animosity in our hearts toward other people. We count on their good will and try our best to work with them. If partnerships do fail, we at least try to make peace before parting company. Judgments in such cases have to be made for practical reasons, they do not touch upon the integrity of the person's guilt or innocence before God.[4]

You cannot give to others that which you do not have. In order to be makers of peace, you must first start with yourself and find some modicum of inner peace. Then you have to try to share that peace with the small circle of people with whom you are closely involved.

For any number of reasons, sometimes you just aren't able to make peace with another person, often a sincere Christian, often a friend, often someone you admire. But at least you can part with good will. What if the other person says, "Get lost. I hate you," or just walks off in a huff? You can still nurture peace in your own heart by praying for that person rather than harboring resentment. You can look forward to resolving your differences—if not in this world, at least in the next, after we have been delivered from the pains and misfortunes of original sin.

You also need to work at becoming more sensitive to the needs of others. Consider especially those who suffer injustice, repression, exploitation, and neglect—those who, unfortunately, must live surrounded by affluence in the land of the free and the home of the brave.

## THE VICTIMS OF INJUSTICE

The little community I belong to, the Franciscans of the Renewal, live in one of the richest and most powerful cities in the world—yet we are surrounded by some of the poorest of the poor. God has especially called us to work with the most helpless and pitiful victims of inequity: impoverished children. These little ones have practically nothing the day they are born and are given precious little in the days and months and years of their struggle to survive. They carry on their small shoulders an unbelievable burden of injustice.

You or someone you know may have been a victim of one of those children. I know many churchgoers who have been mugged, knocked down, hurt, and frightened by some human being who attacked them like a wild animal. I can only urge such victims to look back and see what might make a person behave in such a way. You will inevitably find that these crimes exist because thousands of children are born into a world without hope. I hope you will never be the victim of this anger and hopelessness. But if you ever *do* pay the price of victimization for the world's injustice, try to understand that you have borne painfully a bit of the cross, the same cross under which Jesus fell when he collapsed, exhausted, onto the streets of Jerusalem.

And haven't we all been victims of injustice—through our own doing, and because of others? Injustice is everywhere, though we are often our own worst enemies. Consider all the sorrow that has afflicted your family in the past. Think of all the botched relationships that have wounded you so deeply.

No wonder Christ calls us to pursue peace, to speak up for the cause of justice from which peace comes. As the popes have said in every Christmas message over the last several decades, peace is only possible in a world where there is justice. Cardinal John O'Connor of New York chose this same theme for his motto as bishop: "There is no love without justice."

To be children of God means to spontaneously and freely allow the light of God to shine in our own souls. We don't *cause* peace to reign in our hearts; it comes from within. If we are able to share any kind of peace with others, it is Christ's peace forming us from within. We do the works of God because we have been touched by the Spirit of God.

## WISDOM AND PEACEMAKING

Like mercy and meekness, peace is also considered part of the illuminative way. Those who are able to make and bring peace have already arrived at a higher level of spiritual life. Dr. Muto explains how this peace yields a deeper perspective on the struggles of the purgative way:

The soul illuminated interiorly by the presence of God is truly at peace. This peace makes all the arduous toil of the purgative way seem unimportant. The gift of peace makes the struggle to banish inordinate attachments, distracting thoughts, and ego-centered desires acceptable. God rewards this effort by touches of his ineffable rest. He knows that there soon will be many times when we lose our peace, when we fall back into the old deformative habits of anger, impatience, and useless worry. But we do have to feel confident that we are walking more steadily with the Lord and that he will continue to grant us the gift of peace if we ask him for it. This peace signifies a bond between our restless heart and the heart of Christ in whom we seek our peace.[5]

St. Augustine believed that the peacemakers as well as the persecuted were especially endowed with the gift of wisdom, the greatest of all gifts because it allows us to experience being children of God.[6] Divine wisdom empowers us beyond human means to do the works of God. Wisdom clearly and definitively points us toward eternity in all the struggles of this life.

In explaining the relationship between wisdom and peacemaking, Augustine points out that we will never be delivered from all evil during this life. We hope to be delivered from temptation into which we may fall, but we cannot be exempt from suffering the effects of evil. The gift of wisdom enables us to overcome these effects so that the light of God can help us to press on in our spiritual journey, to walk this difficult pathway of peace.[7] With the surrender of meekness, we live at peace with God and with one another, knowing that we look forward to a better world to come.

## BLESSED ARE THE MARTYRS FOR PEACE

Peacemakers often have a hard time in a warlike world. I once visited Canterbury Cathedral, the site of St. Thomas à

Becket's martyrdom. This twelfth-century Englishman first served as chancellor under Henry II and became his close friend. But when Henry appointed him to be archbishop of Canterbury, Thomas à Becket supported the Church against the monarchy.

The rift between Henry and the archbishop culminated in Thomas à Becket's refusal to approve a constitutional amendment to limit the Church's authority; uncompromising, he was murdered at the entrance to the sanctuary by four knights serving the king's cause. Even though the saint's tomb and relics were destroyed by Henry VIII at the time of the Reformation in an effort to obliterate the churchman's memory, a beautiful memorial now marks the spot of St. Thomas à Becket's death in the cathedral.

To my surprise, I found that a nearby chapel had been transformed into a memorial to the martyrs of the twentieth century. The names of twenty-five or thirty people who had died in the cause of Christ and in the search for peace were inscribed on a stately metal scroll. Some of the names were familiar to me: Edith Stein, Maximilian Kolbe, and Raoul Wallenberg, all of whom died in their struggles against Nazism. Some of these people I had even met, including Martin Luther King, Jr. Other people I had only heard of: an Anglican archbishop who was killed in Africa; members of the Russian Orthodox Church killed during the Russian revolution.

I was especially struck to see a new name printed on a little piece of parchment and taped to the bottom of the scroll: Oscar Romero, Archbishop of El Salvador. Perhaps you have seen *Romero,* the film that tells his story. It may be one of the most moving and yet harrowing motion pictures ever made. This dedicated priest was a gentle and peaceful man who never wanted to become caught up in the middle of a social upheaval. But this became unavoidable. Gradually, the injustice and violence he saw being inflicted upon the poor changed him and his entire approach to his apostolate.

In spite of danger on every side, Archbishop Romero began to move calmly and quietly into the harrowing political conflict. Relentlessly, the film follows his fight against injustice up until the moment of his murder, communicating a sense of inevitability about the tragic outcome. I am told that the archbishop firmly believed that he would meet a violent death at the hands of those who opposed him.

Sad to relate, each of the names on this lengthy scroll in Canterbury Cathedral represents not one hundred, not one thousand, not one million, but many millions of people who have died as innocent victims of war in our century. Most of these people despised war. They wanted nothing more than you and I: to be left in peace. And yet at this writing killing goes on in Lebanon and Israel, in Northern Ireland, in Central America, in Bosnia, in Somalia, in South Africa, in Haiti, and on and on.

Some of the victims commemorated at Canterbury were members of the clergy, some were religious, some were diplomats or government officials, some were heroic doers of good. Most of them, however, were ordinary men and women, including the elderly and the little children caught at the wrong place at the wrong time, victims of the insanity of war. With a spirit of meekness and peace they went to their deaths, and then they came to know that they were indeed the children of God.

If we want to grow in the spiritual life, we must try against all odds to be peacemakers. We need to look for that harbor of peace hidden by grace in our own souls. We need to share peace with those who are dear to us and with those we don't like. We need to forgive our enemies. We need to speak up on behalf of the victims of injustice and neglect.

We need to stand with the immense number of ordinary people in the world who desperately want peace. We need to pray for peace and support those who work for peace by nonviolent means. May we fervently pray for the peace that only

God can give to take root in the hearts of men and women everywhere, and especially in our own.

*Spirit of Wisdom and Spirit of Peace, your sanctuary is hidden in the hearts of those who sincerely seek peace, and your tabernacle is the soul of those who make peace. Along with your presence, given by your gracious generosity, there is much war in my heart. A great storehouse of hurt feelings, of half-forgiven affronts, of bandages from wounds of long ago fills the heart that should be a purified sanctuary glowing with the peaceful light of your presence. When I should find the golden light of wisdom and smell the incense of love, I find only dark shadows and the stench of old wounds. It is no wonder that I cannot make peace with my enemies, my critics, even with my friends and those I love. I am seldom at peace—even when I experience some tranquility because of the absence of distraction.*

*Give me, O Holy Spirit, your gift of wisdom that I may see all other people, in fact all things, in the light of your presence. Move me to remove all the debris of bad memories from your holy temple within. Help me to assist all whom I meet to purge your dwelling place within them that they may find your peace. And when this cleansing is done, or even half done, help me to welcome the Prince of Peace into my heart. Then and only then can I make peace and be called your child. Amen.*

# CHAPTER 9

# The First Beatitude of Union with God: The Power of Poverty

*Blessed are the poor in spirit, for theirs is the kingdom of heaven.*

*T*he life of Mother Henriette Delille is little known because she rarely left New Orleans, the city of her birth. At the turn of the 19th century, while still in her teens, Henriette Delille was called by God to found the Sisters of the Holy Family, an order of black sisters. Defying both social convention and what seemed like human prudence, Mother Delille struggled to establish the religious community, despite opposition that can be attributed to the deeply-rooted social prejudices of that time.

Susan B. Anthony, the famous leader of the women's suffrage movement, paid tribute to the work of this religious community long before the first women's rights convention in 1848: "these negro women had already gone out into the streets, homes, and churches of their city to improve the condition of their race."[1]

When slavery was legal in the United States, Spanish missionaries influenced the authorities of New Orleans to enforce the Spanish code of law concerning slaves, which was less oppressive than the American code. According to Spanish law, children of slaves were not permitted to be separated from their families. It was also much easier for them to obtain their freedom; the laws were so favorable that they established a new class, "free people of color." Those who were only one-quarter black were also sometimes referred to as "quadroons."[2]

This singular class—free people of color, or *gens de couleur libres*—gave New Orleans much of its character, including its reputation for great food, good times, lively music, expert dancing, and refined social graces. It was the only city in the South where rich and poor, black and white, bond and free worshiped together and coexisted in relative peace.

Even so, these "free" people of color still endured a form of social bondage: The women were often induced through financial gain to provide second families for the "soldiers of fortune" who streamed into New Orleans, leaving behind their own families in the North, or in Spain, England, or South America.[3]

Herself both a quadroon and a "free woman of color," Mother Delille courageously faced the prejudice prevalent in that society. Her courage is all the more remarkable given the fact that Mother Delille's fair complexion could have enabled her to "pass" as a white woman, which would have spared her the plight of her darker-skinned sisters. Instead, Henriette chose to identify with them; she became one of the few black heroines to "choose" her race.

The opposition to her work continued long after the order itself was established. Although she considered herself a Catholic religious, Mother Delille spent her adult life unable to wear her habit in public or to legally identify herself as a sister because of segregation laws. Her poverty of spirit and her humility enabled her to continue the primary work of the Sisters of the Holy Family: educating the children of slaves, and generally improving the conditions of all black people and strengthening their faith in Christ and his Church.

The work of the sisters was seen by many whites and blacks alike as openly rebelling against the quadroon tradition, whereby many women of color, as mistresses of the soldiers of fortune, vastly improved their economic circumstances. (The rights of these women and their children were protected by the customs of the city, but their lot was bettered at the peril of their own souls: while true marriages of slaves in New Orleans were recognized by the Church, these illicit unions were not.)

Space does not permit me to tell the whole incredible story here, but you would do well to learn more about this woman of incredible strength coupled with deep humility and poverty of spirit. When Mother Delille died in 1862, she had no idea that her little community of nuns would grow to several hundred members, and would eventually become one of New Orleans most respected institutions. The infamous ballroom where quadroon women met their intended "mates" became an orphanage conducted by her sisters. (More recently, the archbishop of New Orleans has petitioned the Holy See to open her cause of canonization.) The life of Mother Henriette Delille provides ample proof that the kingdom of heaven belongs to the poor in spirit.


DISCIPLES OF MORE

This most confusing of all the Beatitudes—blessed are the poor in spirit—has wound its agonizing way through Church history and through the history of spirituality. Occasional saints such as Francis of Assisi have shed light on it by raising high the banner of poverty. But for the most part, the first Beatitude has been denied, muddled, misunderstood, and rationalized away.

I have heard many people say that Christ doesn't call us to be poor in *fact* but just in *spirit*. Loose translation: "I can have

lots of worldly possessions so long as I really *want* to be poor."
I'm always left wondering exactly *how* they want to be poor, or
in precisely *what* their poverty consists. And in many cases,
these same people eventually give up pretending to be poor
and end up living their lives in search of wealth.

Whatever does it mean to be "poor in spirit"? Before we
attempt to answer that question, let's forget everything we ever
thought we knew on the subject. We must first take a look at
what this puzzling phrase meant to those who heard it two
thousand years ago.

William Barclay's commentary explains that among the Jews
of Jesus' time, two kinds of people were called poor: the dirt
poor and the utterly destitute. The *dirt poor* scratched out a
meager existence from the soil and lived from hand to mouth.
Outside of harvest time, they often had no idea when they
would eat again or where their next meal would come from.[4]

These hard workers usually belonged to a village or a tribe.
They had social roots. And although they were extremely poor,
their membership in a small community of people guaranteed
their basic survival. Many of us who are of European descent
come from this sort of background: our ancestors were peasant
farmers who had little or no money and simply lived from day
to day.

The second kind of poor were the *utterly destitute:* people
with no farm, no regular place to work, and no village. They
simply roamed the city or countryside looking for occasional
work, something to eat, and shelter. Their lack of roots and
community created a much deeper sense of desperation than
did simple hunger. No plot of land, however grubby, stood
between these people and starvation.

We can identify equivalents of these two groups in modern-
day America. Many families and individuals live from week to
week if not from day to day: people on unemployment, people
on welfare, people on a small monthly allotment from Social
Security—just enough to survive. At least in terms of our own

standard of living, these people are definitely poor.

And then we have the utterly destitute: the large numbers of people who walk the streets of New York City—and many other cities as well. Each night they sleep in different churches or shelters for the homeless, receive meals from various social agencies, and continue to wander from here to there not knowing what might be coming next. These people have no land, no home, no possessions other than what they carry on their backs. And many of them have no family other than their comrades on the street.

Now, be completely honest with yourself. Would you volunteer to belong to either group? If you happened to belong to the first group, wouldn't you like to be a bit better off? Most agree with the wry observation of the inimitable Mae West, "I've been poor; I've been rich; rich is better."

Even in the middle of a thriving metropolis like New York City, I've met Latin Americans who seem quite satisfied with their family, their little neighborhood, and an opportunity to earn a decent daily wage. The exciting lure of "more" played out on television may well snag their children or grandchildren, but I have known many old Spanish *abuelas* or grandmothers who feel no great need to escape Spanish Harlem. They kind of like the place.

During the summer of 1968, when many well-meaning suburbanites came to Harlem to lend a helping hand, one elderly black lady said to me, "You know, it is bad enough I'm *poor*; now I've got to be *saved* too! They won't leave me alone." Ordinarily she was one of the happiest people I knew, yet I didn't blame her reaction when crowds kept coming to Harlem, trying to improve her "quality of life" with more enthusiasm than sensitivity. They should have been as happy as she was! I'm grateful when people want to help the poor, but we all can be a little blind to the good that is already there.

## POVERTY OF SPIRIT

When we look at the life of Our Lord, we cannot count him among the absolutely destitute—except at the time of his death. Jesus led the frugal life of a peasant carpenter, which he gave up for the even more frugal life of an itinerant preacher. Even though he owned no home, he did fit into a known occupational group and was usually surrounded by friends, as well as foes. I must assume by looking at Our Lord's life that he can't be calling every Christian to be absolutely destitute, as it applies to physical resources—or spiritual ones.

That said, what could "poor in spirit" mean? Probably the phrase that best captures this idea is being *poor in attitude*. You may wonder how this differs from the rationalization I mentioned earlier: it's fine to have many worldly possessions so long as we really *want* to be poor. Being "poor in attitude" means something much deeper. It connotes a powerful and deeply felt sense of utter destitution, of emptiness, of something close to desperation, of not knowing where you'll find your next mouthful of spiritual food or your next gulp of spiritual breath.

This profound spiritual poverty cuts against the grain of human nature. The worldly spirit exalts impatience and rebellion by which we proclaim our independence from God. In this Beatitude, however, Jesus calls us to live with an entirely different attitude: to be constantly aware of and to acknowledge our absolute poverty and emptiness before God, our utter nakedness before all the world. Not always a pretty sight!

Because poverty of spirit espouses the exact opposite of pride, this Beatitude characterizes people in the third stage of the spiritual life, the unitive way. These seekers of God experience in the depths of their being the truth that they are in fact destitute, empty, poor, weak, nothing. They feel totally bereft of God and yet at the same time know that he is everything for them. They seem to walk above the fray, unaffected by the little inconveniences of life that can so easily cause the rest of us to become impatient or outraged.

Those who are truly poor in spirit glory in the cross of Our Lord Jesus Christ. They consider the crucifix their treasure, their pearl of great price. This is not just words for them, but a reality.

St. Paul captured the essence of poverty of spirit when he spoke of a thorn in his flesh given to keep him from being too elated over his abundance of revelations. Paul was speaking not only about external inconveniences, disabilities, and even persecution but also about the spiritual poverty deep within his heart:

> But he [the Lord] said to me, "My grace is sufficient for you, for power is made perfect in weakness." I will all the more gladly boast of my weaknesses, that the power of Christ may rest upon me. For the sake of Christ, then, I am content with weaknesses, insults, hardships, persecutions, and calamities; for when I am weak, then I am strong.
>
> **2 Corinthians 12:9-10**

Do you have the inner strength to admit that you are poor, even in the face of all your learning and achievements? Let's say you've worked extremely hard to pull your life together and develop a positive self-image as a grace-given child of God. Then someone comes along and tells you that to advance in the spiritual life, you have to be poor in spirit. First you're told that you are a child of God, beloved of the Father and heir to vast riches. And then you hear the next step: now believe that you're utterly destitute. Did you ever get the impression that we Christians are on a very complicated journey?

## OUR PLACE IN THE UNIVERSE

We have to acknowledge our destitution in many ways in order to overcome our natural arrogance as human beings. We each like to think that we're terribly important, even terminally unique, that the whole world should revolve around us. When we gaze into the night sky and observe the familiar stars, we almost feel a sense of ownership.

But do you realize how far away the nearest star actually is? Alpha Centauri is four and a half light years away! When the United States sent a spacecraft out of the solar system, traveling at thousands of miles an hour with no atmosphere to slow it down, the engineers who launched this tiny craft knew it would take twenty-four thousand years to sail to the nearest star—some ten and a half times the length of the Christian era. Isn't that fantastic? How little we really are.

Living for what seems to be a very long time, you and I can feel so important in our own small sphere of influence. Yet in reality, we are a like tiny mayflies that are here today and gone tomorrow. Of minuscule importance in terms of time and space, we inhabit this world in the most temporary way. When we look up at the stars, we can rightly only shake our heads in wonderment. "What is man that thou art mindful of him, and the son of man that thou dost care for him?" (Ps 8:4).

Did you ever stop to think how little we are even in terms of our human environment? We make our home not in the vastness of space, but in this limited world of human beings. We each know and are known by a certain number of people: our relatives, friends, neighbors, bosses, those who work with us and for us, our children's teachers the lady in the local delicatessen, the waiter at our favorite restaurant, the cashier at the nearby supermarket, perhaps the hairdresser or barber who has served us for years.

That is our little world. Yet we are in fact awash in a great ocean of people. When our lives come to an end, some people will grieve, but most of them will never have even been aware of our existence. As far as this world is concerned, we march from obscurity to oblivion.

I spent one summer teaching in Sydney, Australia, where a

small finger of the Pacific Ocean courses right into the middle of the city. If you take a short walk to the cliffs which surround the ocean, you can peer over a guardrail to the beach a thousand feet below. Children playing in the sand look like tiny insects. Peering out over the vast expanse of the ocean reveals nothing but water, as far as the eye can see. It seems like a vast solitude.

Nevertheless, we know for a fact that a fantastic universe lies directly beneath the surface: great whales, billions of fish, unthinkable creatures of all shapes and sizes swimming in the dark depths of this liquid abyss. Are the children who splash in the shallow water aware of this teeming assortment of life not so far away? Not at all.

In its own way, humanity is like a vast ocean. Twenty-five generations ago, about five hundred years, you alone have had two hundred and seventy-one thousand direct ancestors. How many do you know anything about? In the same way, twenty-five generations from now—if we haven't succeeded in blowing up the earth by then—in all probability people looking back on our time will not remember you among *their* two hundred and seventy-one thousand ancestors living at this time.

How insignificant we are, like ants in an ant hill or microbes under a microscope. Only one thing saves us from meaningless oblivion: "You hast made him little less than God, and dost crown him with glory and honor." (Ps 8:5).

The only reason human life doesn't reduce itself to a cruel and bitter joke is God's immense generosity. He has made us different from all of the other creatures by giving each of us a soul with an eternal destiny. Beyond all human understanding, God has reached out of his infinity into our microscopic existence and called us to himself. By the mysterious reality of divine grace, he has made us his children.

I believe that only the poor in spirit know how truly rich they are. Aware of their infinitesimal tininess, only those who have opened their hearts to God in the very depths of their being know what it is to be a child of God.

St. Francis often remarked that if people only knew what abundant spiritual riches were theirs, they would throw everything else away. They would count it all junk if they could just possess a little bit more of that internal treasure, riches given by divine grace that cannot be purchased by any amount of silver or gold.

## A WINDOW INTO INFINITY

In several of his writings, Fr. Adrian Van Kaam explains what it is that leads us along the path of obedience to God and to reverential love and poverty of spirit: the recognition of our total dependency, of our utter aloneness, of our absolute vulnerability.[5] Whether we look up at the stars, or look under the ocean, or shake our heads over the vast scope of the human race, we realize that all of life can show us something of the infinite goodness of God, and of our total poverty without him. Van Kaam calls this experience self alienation. It is an essential step on the spiritual journey.

What happens when you try to look into yourself? You discover that the largest universe and the deepest ocean reside right inside your own heart and mind. In fact, the sky and the sea are small compared to what is inside you. Why? Because the sky will perish and the sea will dry up and the world will come to nothing, but inside you God has placed a soul, a window into infinity. And when you peer into that window by prayer and meditation, with the help of divine grace, then you begin to see what you truly are.

Oh, the immensity of the human soul! Yet what poor creatures we are, and how humbling it is to recognize that we so often fail to make use of the eternal riches within. I first gave this conference on the Beatitudes in the Capuchin church of St. John the Baptist on Thirtieth Street in Manhattan. This stately old sanctuary contains a few beautiful religious antiques, including a marvelous old marble seat for the priest who presides. On the day I was to speak on this particular Beatitude, I thought to myself, *All these people have come here to listen to you talk about poverty of spirit. You're going to sit up in front of them on the ancient bench that comes down from the Middle Ages, that beautiful stone chair several hundred years old, and tell them to be poor in spirit. And they're going to say to themselves, "What does he know about being poor in spirit? He's a priest, somebody people listen to, someone people tip their hats to. What does he know about being poor in spirit?"*

I sometimes look into my soul in the early light of dawn—when my mind is uncluttered by the demands of the day. I find only unspeakable poverty, wretchedness, misery, and sinfulness—a misery accentuated by my priestly role and duties. Whenever I perform the sacramental rites that draw me so close to the bright fires of grace, I feel like a moth fearful of being drawn into the flame.

A bishop must feel poorer still when he thinks about serving as one of the chief shepherds of the Church. Many of the bishops I know feel very unworthy, terribly humbled, deeply overwhelmed by their personal poverty in relationship to their vocation.

And how humiliating the papacy must be! How alarming to stand as pope in the gray light of dawn. An old Italian proverb sums up the steep price of spiritual leadership: "Heavy hangs the great mantle on the shoulders of him who would guard it from the mud." I believe this reality took the life of John Paul I. He was such a humble man that I don't think he could live with his awesome calling.

No one is exempt from the need to become poor in spirit. To do so, we must look into our own souls and see all the graces unused or wasted, all the gifts unaccepted, all the calls to do good left unheeded. With God's help, this recognition will bring a solitary sense of absolute destitution, of self alienation, of poverty of spirit.

I once told Mother Teresa that I felt humiliated because I failed in a task I was given to do, and that I regretted never having really been humbled. She replied, "Well, cheer up. Humiliation can be a road to humility." And to poverty of spirit.

## GROWING IN WISDOM

How blessed are the poor in spirit. Why? Because the kingdom of heaven is theirs. St. Augustine says that God teaches us to be poor in spirit especially by the gift of wisdom.[6] With this gift we learn how to evaluate everything around us in light of the kingdom of God—all our gifts, talents, failures, possibilities, joys, and sorrows.

How can you begin to receive more of God's wisdom about what it means to be poor in spirit? If, like myself, you are among the vast majority who are not yet walking in the unitive way, how can you begin to live out this awesome calling?

The first thing I would suggest is to try a little make-believe poverty of spirit. Alcoholics Anonymous offers a piece of advice to those who feel overwhelmed at the prospect of giving up drinking: "act as if," or "fake it 'til you make it." I think that same kind of advice could be applied here. As with most of Christ's commands, we must grow into these size-fourteen shoes before we will be able to walk comfortably.

Now, I'm not saying *pretend* to look humble; I'm suggesting that by *acting* humbly, you might *become* humble. The account of Mother Delille offers an excellent case in point. She suffered all this injustice and actively worked to bring it to an end. She must have become outraged, and yet she never complained. Why? Because she was poor in spirit.

If you want a litmus test to see if your own poverty of spirit is authentic and growing, I suggest you ask yourself the following questions.

**Do you try to detach yourself from a sense of ownership?**
Do you disengage yourself from the material things you possess, like your car, your house, your furniture—or do you often find them at the center of your attention? Do you feel a certain detachment from other aspects of life: your work, your special talents, your personal income, your health, your time, your dreams for the future, even your charitable endeavors? Even more importantly, do you detach yourself from much more precious or beloved parts of your life: your spouse, your children, your special friends?

Love for family and friends can often give us the courage to detach ourselves from worldly power or possessions. Only suffering, however, can help us become detached from those we love. I've seen parents who have lost a child to an illness or an accident completely reorder their life priorities—but only after finally accepting the fact that God had permitted them to lose for a time someone they loved so much.

We must always leave the hand of God free, even in the purest of affections. Poverty of spirit demands that we endure with some measure of peace the sorrow of losing a loved one, even though we will someday be reunited in the kingdom of heaven. If detachment doesn't teach us to keep a loose grip on family and friends, then we will go through life terrified by the prospect of losing those we love. And if we cling too tightly, then we will in all likelihood drive them away.

Our involvement in a parish or religious community or good work demands a similar detachment. We don't need to be constantly dwelling on death or sorrow or separation, but we do need to go through life having accepted the fact that *every* good thing in this world will come to an end. Among the spiritual treasures that Scripture says will endure forever is the reward of poverty of spirit. We can be sure that this will not reach an eventual dead end, because those who practice it are promised the kingdom of God.

A sense of detachment means that we love and enjoy and

appreciate all that we have, *but that we give it all back to God.*
Poverty of spirit also means that we try to avoid selfishness and
overindulgence. Worldliness and Christian discipleship mix
about as well as oil and water. The tendency to use and enjoy
things, even prayer and spiritual consolations, apart from any
reference to God's will remains a constant trap for all of us.
Even in situations where we seem to be on the brink of losing
everything, detachment teaches us that we do not lose things
which are eternal, like the mercy of God.

**Are you willing to part with some of your hard-earned
goods for those who are in need?** A helpful barometer of
poverty of spirit is to examine whether or not we practice generosity in various ways. We should be eternally grateful to the
poor and needy, those impoverished souls who serve as a mir-
ror of our poverty before God.

Without God, each and every one of us is poorer than the
most destitute person on this earth. The imperious millionaire
waiting impatiently in his fancy limousine for the chauffeur to
open his car door may not realize how impoverished he really
is—until it catches up with him on the psychiatrist's couch or
in the doctor's office.

One absurdity of our human condition is that the poor man
and the rich man can be equally foolish in different ways.
Consider the beggar in rags who stands on the sidewalk and
watches our millionaire climb out of his sleek limousine. The
beggar can be consumed by desperate jealousy. The chauffeur
might be the only person in this scenario who knows how poor
the rich man really is!

We see in this caricature how the Beatitudes can highlight
the inherent paradoxes of life. While the beggar may be rich in
desire and the rich man may be impoverished in his foolish
reliance on possessions, the chauffeur who is poor in spirit may
be truly rich in the kingdom of heaven.

I certainly don't mean to imply that all wealthy people fail to practice poverty of spirit, or that all poor people fall prey to jealousy. As I mentioned earlier, I have known many of the poor who are quite content; I have likewise met many of the wealthy who are quite generous and unimpressed with their assets. And I have also met many of the rest of us who are neither rich nor destitute but who are not so poor in spirit.

**Do you feel the kingdom of God coming in your own soul?** The first question concerning our detachment from material possessions and relationships is simple enough. The second one reflecting on our generosity is a bit more disturbing. But this third question provides the acid test for how poor we really are in spirit.

Despite your destitution, your weakness, your distractions, your inner stresses and strains, do you feel the kingdom of God unfolding within you? You should, wherever you may be on your spiritual journey.

Not that this internal unfolding of the kingdom will necessarily feel like a beautiful rose opening in the morning sun, with each delicate petal touched by the dew. In reality, a great many Christians feel more like an untidy ball of yarn unwinding bit by bit, as if it were being batted about by a mischievous kitten, or like a knitted sweater becoming unraveled.

The fortunate ones among us may detect something profoundly spiritual deep within, be it ever so faint. In any case, you will know that the kingdom of God is coming in your own soul because it calls you to grow in holiness. Each day it will call you to take one more little step toward God. And when you don't take that step, the kingdom of God will feel a bit like heartburn, a gnawing pain that will continue to bother you no matter what you do. This summons of the kingdom will keep knocking on the door of your heart until you say yes.

Even if you are just starting out on your spiritual journey, you have already begun to know a little bit about what it means to be poor in spirit. Dr. Muto writes of the blessings that come to us through this work of grace in our souls:

> From a human viewpoint, poverty of spirit enables us to regain our freedom, to be who we really are: dependent, solitary, vulnerable creatures who are blessed in this knowledge, and on the basis of it pursue transcendent meaning, loving relations, noble achievement for the common good. Because we possess nothing ultimately, we can and do become poor companions of everyone and everything. Without poverty of spirit we become predators. With poverty of spirit we are the caretakers.[7]

You will also know the kingdom of God is coming within you if you have regard for the poor whom you meet along the way. For the most part, the nobility of many of the poor and the depth of their patient suffering is recognized only by those few who are close to God.

One practical way to grow in poverty of spirit is to spend time with people who are already living this Beatitude themselves. I remember sharing lunch with one such person: Fr. Patrick Peyton, founder of the Family Rosary Movement. This humble, prayerful man died at the ripe old age of eighty-three, having preached to millions of people over the course of his lifetime. Fr. Peyton would never have admitted it, but you could tell immediately that he was poor in spirit.

Fr. Peyton would speak in the most poignant and moving way of his simple roots, of the little farm where his devout parents had raised their family. He was a friend of many famous people, political leaders, and people in the media, but he always approached them in the most humble and open way. And they invariably responded with heartfelt affection and gratitude, grateful that this godly man was coming to ask their help.

## AN IMPOVERISHED LOVER OF GOD

One of my favorite examples of poverty of spirit is an ex-seminarian named Francis Thompson. I once visited the seminary he attended, Ushaw College outside of Durham, England. I took time to study the large number of portraits lining the walls of the vestibule.

Nearest the entrance hang paintings of the early apostolic vicars of England, missionaries who persevered in the face of persecution. Then come the first public bishops in England after the Catholic Emancipation Act, a law enacted in 1829 which removed most of the civil penalties imposed on British Roman Catholics.

Farther along hang huge, formal portraits of bishops more elegantly robed as would become the English aristocracy. These prelates, right down to our times, are rather impressive in appearance. (Most of them were good men I'm sure, and no doubt many of them were poor in spirit despite their aristocratic attire.)

Way down at the end of the corridor, I found a little picture the size of a postcard that had been placed in a larger frame so that it wouldn't be lost in this impressive collection. A closer look revealed the saddest, sickliest-looking sixteen-year-old boy I had ever seen in my life. He looked like he needed vitamin $B_{12}$ shots, and like he didn't have a friend in the world. Underneath the portrait is written "Francis Thompson," the name of a man whom some of us consider one of the greatest religious poets in the English language.

Thompson entered the seminary around 1870, but the rector eventually decided this artistic soul wasn't meant to be a priest. Floundering about to find his calling, Thompson studied medicine for a while, failed as a salesman, was rejected by the army, and finally turned to opium after his mother's death. Eight years later, when Thompson himself was near death, an editor sought out the poet and sent him to a sanatorium. Once he was cured of his drug addiction, this poetic genius began to write and publish in earnest.

For many years of his life, however, Francis Thompson was numbered among the destitute of society. Disowned by his family because of his opium addiction, he would spend many a chilly night on a park bench near London's Picadilly Circus, a bustling area of shops and restaurants. As he looked out at the Thames River, this impoverished beholder of beauty would write his poems on little pieces of paper.

This destitute poet had no place to rest his head other than a park bench, yet he possessed something of the kingdom of heaven. That same miracle can happen to you.

Right near Picadilly Circus, the Thames River is spanned by a very old bridge and monument called The Charing Cross. As Francis Thompson sat there, he described how the kingdom of God can come to someone who was so desperately poor. Indeed, he was able to see God all around him.

Oh world invisible, we view thee,
Oh world intangible, we touch thee,
Oh world unknowable, we know thee,
Inapprehensible, we clutch thee!

Does the fish soar to find the ocean,
The eagle plunge to find the air—
That we ask of the stars in motion
If they have rumour of thee there?

Not where the wheeling systems darken,
And our benumbed conceiving soars!—
The drift of pinions, would we hearken,
Beats at our own clay-shuttered doors.

The angels keep their ancient places;—
Turn but a stone and start a wing!

'Tis ye, 'tis your estranged faces,
That miss the many splendoured thing.

But when so sad thou canst not sadder
Cry; and upon thy so sore loss
Shall shine the traffic of Jacob's ladder
Pitched betwixt Heaven and Charing Cross.

Yea, in the night, my Soul, my daughter,
Cry, clinging Heaven by the hems;
And lo, Christ walking on the water
Not of Gennesareth, but Thames![8]

Wilfred Meynell, himself a Catholic poet and writer, was the editor of Thompson's works; he and his wife, Alice, were also Thompson's friends. Meynell puts this revealing footnote after the poem:

> This poem (found among his papers when he died) Francis Thompson might yet have worked to remove, here a defective rhyme, there an unexpected elision. But no altered mind would he have brought to the purport of it; the prevision of "Heaven in Earth and God in Man" pervading his earlier published verse, is here accented by poignantly local and personal allusion. For in these triumphing stanzas he held in retrospect those days and nights of human dereliction he spent beside London's River, and in the shadow—but all radiance to him—of Charing Cross.[9]

As Francis Thompson looked out on the Thames River flowing through the great city of London, he was so alone—the particular aloneness you can experience only in the midst of a crowd of strangers. But when this gentle poet walked over to the railing, he saw a divine presence upon the water. And he was no longer alone.

You too can catch a glimpse of the kingdom of heaven. Embrace your inner poverty. Let it change your life. Let it temper your limitations and shortcomings as they come more and more into view. Let it help you to accept aging or sickness or failure. And then in the darkness across the water will come the only Presence which lasts forever.

⁓

*Holy Spirit, you create all things and all is yours. Yet you are so silent, so hidden that we never think of your supreme possession and disposition of all the universe. You, together with the Father and Son create all things, rule over all, and summon all to you as our final goal. Deliver us by your wisdom in which all things are made, from all foolish thoughts of possessions and exclusiveness. Let us ever be mindful that we are stewards of all we have until the Master returns. May wisdom teach us to be generous, detached, joyous in giving, and careful in receiving. But most of all, Spirit of Wisdom, call on our hearts by joy and sorrow, in good times and in bad, that we may always seek first that kingdom that never passes away. Amen.*

# CHAPTER 10

# The Second Beatitude of Union with God: Seeing through a Glass Darkly

*Blessed are the pure in heart, for they shall see God.*

## A JEWISH SAINT

The recent beatification of Edith Stein brought together the history of Israel and the mystery of the cross. For Christians of all denominations, this courageous woman provides a powerful example of a person who refused to cooperate with evil.

This incredibly rich story can be told with deceptively few and simple facts. Edith was born in 1891 to a Jewish family in Germany, and graduated summa cum laude with her doctorate in philosophy from Freiburg University in 1916. Edith once described herself as an atheist, yet she was also a passionate seeker of truth. Her first encounter with Christian truth occurred when she read the Lord's Prayer. After a period of profound inner conflict, Edith came across the autobiography of St. Teresa of Avila and stayed up most of the night reading it. Having been brought to the threshold of the Catholic Church through Teresa's writings, this learned woman was baptized on January 1, 1922, and confirmed the following month.

After a decade of teaching in Catholic schools and lecturing on philosophical and spiritual subjects, Edith Stein entered the Carmelite convent of Cologne on October 14, 1933. There she became known as Sr. Benedicta of the Cross. This joyous event occurred against a backdrop of intense conflict and turmoil: Edith's mother was grief-stricken by this decision, and it cost Edith dearly to leave her. At a time when Nazi anti-Semitism was building with alarming speed, she understandably perceived her daughter's new identity as a rejection of her Jewish heritage. In fact, Sr. Benedicta was very loyal to her people; her refusal to deny them would ultimately lead her to the gas chamber at Auschwitz.

The vast majority of believing Christians in Germany came to despise all that the Nazis stood for, but many went along at first. They presumed that Hitler could not last; they also faced the likelihood of punishment or even death if they mounted any resistance. A plebiscite in 1939 required all eligible citizens to vote. Of course, they were "encouraged" to give their stamp of approval to the Führer. Hilda Graef, in her biography of Edith Stein entitled *The Scholar and the Cross*, describes the debate that ensued at the Carmelite convent:

> Many monasteries of both men and women had already been closed, and the religious had been literally driven into the street. Some well-meaning people had advised the nuns not to vote at all, but they had never done that before since they had permission to leave the enclosure for the purpose....
> The majority of the nuns were of the opinion that they

should vote for Hitler so as to avoid any repercussions, for it was well-known in Germany that the voting was not secret and failure to give one's vote to the Führer had most serious consequences. In addition, the nuns contended that it did not matter anyway how they voted; the result of these elections was a foregone conclusion. In fact, everyone knew that it was going to be about 98 percent for the Führer....

This view, however, was violently opposed by Sr. Benedicta. She, otherwise so gentle and quick to give way, could hardly be recognized. Again and again, she urged the sisters not to vote for Hitler, no matter what the consequences for the individual or the community. He was an enemy of God and would drag Germany to ruin with him.[1]

As it turned out, the election committee arrived on the doorstep of the convent that very morning to collect the nuns' ballots. In the process, they discovered that Edith Stein was not an Aryan. From then on, she was a marked person. The Nazis continued their pursuit even after her superiors transferred Sr. Benedicta to the safety of a Carmelite convent in Holland. The Dutch bishops vehemently protested any deportation of Jews. Nevertheless, the Nazi government soon arrested all Catholics with any known Jewish ancestry.

Graef details Edith Stein's arrival at the Auschwitz concentration camp in 1942. Days later, she and her sister were sent to the gas chambers, to be counted among the millions of innocent people who were destined to die during the Holocaust.

Among the prisoners who arrived on August 5, Sr. Benedicta made a striking impression by her great calm and composure. The misery in the camp and the excitement among the newcomers were indescribable. Sr. Benedicta walked about among the women, comforting, helping, soothing like an angel.

Many mothers were almost demented and had for days not been looking after their children, but had been sitting, brooding in listless despair. Sr. Benedicta at once took care of the poor little ones, washed and combed them, and saw to it that they got food and attention. As long as she was in the camp she made washing and cleaning one of her principal charitable activities, so that everyone was amazed. [2]

Throughout the good times and the bad, Edith Stein demonstrated a passion for truth. This burning desire guided her study of philosophy and eventually led her to embrace Catholicism, a faith about which she had known practically nothing. Her passion for truth gave her the strength to become a Carmelite nun at the very time when she was most torn by the rise of anti-Semitism. This same passion inspired her to dispute the wisdom of voting for Adolf Hitler, and finally to remain loyal to Christ in the face of death.

## WHAT DOES IT MEAN TO BE PURE OF HEART?

The zealous pursuit of truth is one of the most important aspects of purity of heart. It is also an essential element of growth in the spiritual life, especially at its highest dimension: the unitive way. We cannot hope to draw close to God without being seekers of truth. "Blessed are the pure of heart, for they shall see God."

Those of us who are still struggling along the earlier stages of the spiritual journey have much to learn from this Beatitude. God never speaks his word in order to hit us over the head with unattainable commands. Rather, he wants to instruct our finite minds, to purify our conflicted hearts, and to reassure our drooping spirits.

This Beatitude first indicates how we can lengthen our strides along the spiritual path: we must grow in purity of heart. When Our Lord spoke these words, he probably used a Hebrew phrase quite familiar to most New Yorkers. On the window of every Jewish butcher shop, a sign repeats the word twice: *kosher, kosher.* This double use of the Hebrew term means the butcher sells only what is strictly kosher or pure, meat that has been ritually slaughtered and carefully preserved according to the Jewish laws. When Jesus spoke of purity of heart, he used this same significant word: *kosher.*

The same term can be applied to the character and soul of a person. I once heard a rabbi say that only Jews are obliged to keep a kosher table, but all people are obliged to have a "kosher heart," a character that is pure. The New Testament, written in Greek, translates this Hebrew word as *katharos,* which also means "clean" or "purified." The English word "cathartic" comes from the same root.[3]

On the eve of Passover, Orthodox Jews purge their homes of every last bit of food containing any leavening or yeast. (Happy beneficiaries of their labors are never hard to find. On one such occasion, the rabbi's wife came to our retreat house with bags of food for us to give to the poor, along with large plastic containers of soups and casseroles made with dairy products.)

In order for their houses to be absolutely pure, the Jews also have to wash all their dishes and silverware in water three times. The rabbi's wife asked me in jest, "Wouldn't you think we could catch up with the electric dishwasher?" But all of these customs have insured ritual purity for the Jews for centuries.

As an aside, let me share a funny story that this lively Jewish lady couldn't resist telling me about their own Passover preparations. They happened to overhear their cook, a Baptist woman, as she dunked the silverware into the sink in her own special way. Since each item had to be immersed three times, she was chanting rhythmically with each dunk, "In the name of the Father, and the Son, and the Holy Ghost." Only in

America with its incredible mixture of cultures and religions! Such humorous encounters must make the Lord himself chuckle.

The terms *kosher* and *katharos* can also be applied to other types of cleaning, chores which need to be done with some regularity. For instance, is your house ever so perfectly clean that you don't have to work at it anymore? Whoever finds a way to accomplish that trick could make a fortune. Or consider a more personal example: is your body ever so perfectly groomed that you will never have to take care of it again? Suppose I said to my barber, "George, that's such a wonderful haircut that it'll do me for the rest of my life! I'll see you on the other side of the grave." We know that these sorts of procedures are never permanent. In this world, we are constantly cleaning, constantly grooming.

Cleanliness of heart is like that, too. Spiritual purity is not a static condition, an ultimate goal at which we can ever arrive in this life. Rather, it is something for which we constantly labor. *Why* do we face such a continuing struggle? Because we are human beings, fallen creatures whose minds need to be cleansed of worldly perceptions, whose hearts need to be cleansed of base desires.

We are rather like the Jewish home on the eve of Passover that needs to be searched and purified of anything offensive to God. And after having been purged, our minds and hearts need to be immersed in God's truth for a long soak to wash away any residue of the world's filth.

Sometimes our minds and hearts require just a routine cleaning. At other times we may face a much bigger job, perhaps like the effort required to clean up a house after a fire or flood. Unfortunately, these times of more serious impurity tend to creep up on us when we fail to notice that our spiritual household is falling into disorder. The effects of fire and flood are obvious to the naked eye; signposts along the spiritual pathway are a lot harder to read.

Consider as a case in point the Carmelite sisters, who thought they should vote for Hitler despite their horror at what he was doing. These were devout women, but circumstances had put tremendous pressure on them. One might argue that Sr. Benedicta's Jewish background enabled her to see things more clearly. But the fact is that she *did* see the truth, for whatever reason. Many heroic Christians in Germany did refuse to voice any support for Hitler, and many paid with their lives. But the great majority went along, however reluctantly, and ended up with a huge amount of debris in their own spiritual houses.

Mind you, I'm not saying that I would have acted any differently. What I am saying is that we should recognize and admire the wisdom of those who refused to be swept along in the floodwaters of spiritual darkness. We should allow ourselves to be instructed and inspired by those who demonstrated such purity of heart.

## PURITY OF HEART GOES DEEPER AND DEEPER

"Purity of heart" can be separated into three different facets: purity of perception, of understanding, and of desire. Jesus is speaking of *purity of perception* when he says, "The eye is the lamp of the body. So, if your eye is sound, your whole body will be full of light; but if your eye is not sound, your whole body will be full of darkness. If then the light in you is darkness, how great is the darkness!" (Mt 6:22-23).

The human eye can perceive an immense number of individual objects in the course of a single day. But what do we really perceive at the depths of our being? Suppose a young woman dressed in a provocative outfit strolls through the local park. A man sitting on a nearby bench sees a seductive enchantress; another is vaguely aware that a stranger is passing by. A taxi driver sees a potential customer. The young woman's father sees his beloved little girl, while her boyfriend sees the most beautiful woman in the world. A prudish spinster sees only an object of disgust.

People receiving the same visual input may have quite dissimilar perceptions. This young woman becomes for different observers a temptress, a shadow, a possible taxi fare, a beloved child, a potential spouse, or a shameful harlot. A seeker of truth may perceive something entirely different, seeing only a child of God who is in danger of being misled and claimed by a pagan culture—and say a prayer for her.

*Purity of understanding* goes deeper. It does not simply perceive: it comprehends things, or at least tries to understand them in the light of God's love. St. Augustine linked the spiritual gift of understanding with this Beatitude of a pure heart. The Holy Spirit wants to give us insight far beyond our own natural powers of perception. As we come to know the mind of God, we become less governed by the flesh, less oblivious to others, less preoccupied with monetary gain, less naïve, less selfish, less judgmental. We simply grow in compassion and purity of heart.

We also gradually come to see "with a cleansed eye" what eye has not seen, nor ear heard, nor has entered into the heart of man—the kingdom of God. Augustine observed that the physical eye cannot see this kingdom because it has no color, nor can the ear hear it because it makes no sound, nor can it enter into the heart because the heart must enter into it.[4]

Recently, a young man imprisoned for shooting a New York City police officer about ten years ago was mistakenly released and then rearrested the next day. The officer he shot happens to be a friend of mine named Stephen McDonald, a man who has been severely paralyzed for the past decade as a result of his gunshot wounds.

A local newspaper reported Steve as saying that he understood how disappointed this young man must have been to be sent back to prison. He also commended the gunman's grandmother, a devout woman who had supported her grandson throughout this sad affair. Steve's words demonstrated purity of heart. The gift of understanding has allowed him to appreciate the feelings of someone who, according to the world's standards, should be his mortal enemy. My friend will be incapacitated for the rest of his life, but by faith and grace he has become an example of courage and compassion to those who know him. But such understanding is not easy to come by. It is a gift of the Holy Spirit which must be received.

The deepest dimension of a pure heart is *purity of desire*, something even more difficult to achieve. In order for our desires to become pure, we have to lose things—a prospect that doesn't make us tingle with the joy of anticipation. But without suffering the loss of whatever keeps us from knowing God more fully, we will never achieve that union for which we were created.

## FROM CRADLE TO GRAVE

As I pointed out at the beginning of this book, the spiritual life is a constant process of giving up lesser goods for greater goods. We spend our lives locked in armed combat with ourselves, struggling constantly to let go of that which we no longer need, of that which keeps us from seeing God.

This weaning process begins early in life. When we were little, our mothers fed us pablum and baby food to wean us from the breast or bottle. After we had a few teeth, she had to deny us processed baby food to get us onto solids. As toddlers, we felt secure at home with our own toys and siblings. But then came that heart-rending day when we had to go to kindergarten or first grade. Perhaps you were one of the brave ones, but most of us cried. Going out into the big world can seem so frightening to a small child. I remember very clearly the excitement and the fear of my first day in school.

And so we continue throughout our lives, giving up not only the bad but also that which is no longer relevant or helpful for our spiritual growth. This cleansing process can be extremely painful—a sort of spiritual surgery that none of us could survive apart from divine grace. Thank God we don't have to do it on our own.

Have you ever tried to make a list of all the things you've lost in the course of your life? As someone no longer in his prime, I'm discovering that not only is my hair starting to disappear but also my health and my vitality. As I grow older, I'm hopefully growing wiser, but I'm certainly growing physically weaker and drawing nearer to the day of my departure from this earth—the final purification. I think we should take care not to shorten the days God has granted us, but I for one hope to embrace that final purification of bodily death with all the zeal I can muster.

As I mentioned in the first chapter, certain aspects of our lives can be extraordinarily good. They may even have something about them that will last forever—but they themselves will not. These are called *contingent goods*. For example, perhaps you live in a comfortable and spacious farmhouse, the perfect place for raising children. You're going to lose it sooner or later. Maybe you're married to someone you deeply love, or belong to a close-knit parish, or enjoy a few lasting friendships. Sooner or later you will lose each one of these people who means so much to you. Don't be surprised or afraid—at least not too afraid.

Even Jesus, who loved with the purest of hearts, had to go through this purification process. He suffered the loss of his childhood home in Nazareth. No group of people was ever purer than the Holy Family, yet even that came to an end. According to tradition, Joseph died when Christ was still at home. In fact, we look to him as the patron of a happy death. And when Joseph departed from this earth, I feel sure that Mary and Jesus wept for him. After all, they were perfectly human.

As the purest man who ever lived, did Jesus himself remain in this world? Not in his earthly body. Mary had to endure the fearsome and painful agony of watching the crucifixion of her son—he who was most innocent. And so the Holy Family was finally reduced to one old woman, an enigmatic figure no one could completely understand. Mary had known and experienced things that no one else ever had. And in silence she had to await her own passing for many years. We call Mary Our Lady of Sorrows because she had to lose everything. You might find it a great help to pray to her as you gradually relinquish everything in your own life.

You can go through this purification process in one of two ways: kicking and screaming, or calmly and quietly. You can grasp angrily that which you hold dear and hurl your fury heavenward, or you can let it go—sadly and tearfully perhaps, but with a deep inner peace because you understand that God is loving you as only a perfect Father can.

Which do you want? Either way you will eventually lose everything. But if you gradually let go in peace, you will receive purity of heart in return. And each step toward purity of heart will allow you to take one more step on your spiritual journey, to grow closer to the heart and desires of God.


## PEACE IN THE MIDST OF PAIN

Even in the worst of circumstances, a person who has surrendered all to God, who is prepared to lose all so as to find all (to use the words of St. John of the Cross), will have an inner composure. Someone who observed Edith Stein shortly before her death remarked on this:

> My personal impression is that she was most deeply sorrowful but without anxiety. I cannot express it better than by saying that she gave the impression of bearing such an enor-

mous load of sorrow that even when she did smile, it only made one more sorrowful. She hardly ever spoke, but she often looked at her sister Rosa with indescribable sadness.... She was thinking of the sorrow she foresaw, not her own sorrow, for that she was far too calm; she thought of the sorrow that awaited the others. Her whole appearance, as I picture her in my memory sitting in that hut, suggested only one thought to me: a Pietà without Christ.[5]

Have you ever imagined a person who has reached a high level of this third unitive way as an emotionless stoic, someone so detached from the things of this earth as to be seemingly without feelings or humanity? This picture is far from reality. Consider these impressions of a German soldier named Johannes Wieners, who had a chance encounter with Edith Stein a few days before her death:

On the seventh of August, 1942, he and the others in his unit were standing in the switching area of the railroad depot in Breslau since their engine had been uncoupled for servicing. A freight train pulled into the station on the track next to theirs. A minute or so later, a guard opened a sliding door on one of the cars. With dismay, Wieners noticed it was packed with people who were jammed together, cowering on the floor. The stench coming from the car almost overpowered the men standing outside.

Then a woman in nun's clothing stepped into the opening. Wieners looked at her with such commiseration that she spoke to him: "It's awful. We have nothing by way of containers for sanitation needs." Looking into the distance and then across the town, she said, "This is my beloved hometown. I will never see it again."

When he looked at her, questioningly, she added, very hesitantly: "We are riding to our death."

He was profoundly shocked and asked, in all seriousness:

"Do your companion prisoners believe that also?"

Her answer came even more hesitantly, "It's better that they do not know it."

Wieners' companions were irritated that he spoke to a Jewess and berated him for it. But one of them who had overheard the conversation joined him. The two men discussed quietly in the face of their angry comrades the possibility of doing anything for the people.

Edith had overheard the objections. When they asked her whether they could get her and her companions anything to eat or drink, she replied, "No, thank you, we accept nothing."

The markings on the car made it plain that it had come from Holland. By this time, the boiler on their engine had been refilled, and the locomotive recoupled. The men had to board their train, which then left Breslau station.[6]

Sr. Benedicta of the Cross may have had the appearance of composure, but I have no doubt that she was filled with the deepest of human emotions. Her concern seemed to be directed not so much to her own pain but to the misery of her companions, those who lacked an understanding of their inhumane treatment and their certain fate. But purity of heart gave Edith Stein eyes to see the most awful things imaginable, and still remain close to God.

For most of us who live in more ordinary circumstances, the best way to take small steps toward our final hope of union with God is to use and enjoy the good things he gives us, but to be always ready to surrender them, to relinquish them, to hand them over—whenever God tells us it is time to do so.

As we go through this process of being made pure of heart, we will find a growing capacity to differentiate among the things God asks us to relinquish. We will know which ones are passing and which are everlasting. The Holy Spirit will help us to travel this highest way partly by means of the spiritual gift of understanding, a supernatural discernment that enables us to sort out what God seems to be calling us to surrender.

Yet the hallmark of those seekers of truth who are struggling to grow in purity of heart is *hope*—not that they will never lose anything, but that some lasting good will come out of whatever they do lose. Their readiness and willingness to lose whatever and whomever they truly love comes out of their firm belief that they will eventually find these goods again.

Therein lies one of the great secrets of holiness. Each of us will eventually come to the end of our days. And when we do approach the portals of death, those of us who have sincerely tried to grow in purity of heart will be able to gently and peacefully lay everything aside. We will be able to say to the Lord, "Into thy hands I commend my spirit."

## FINDING GOD EVEN IN THE LOSING

Some people go around looking glum all the time. They make every day seem like Good Friday as they cast a pall of doom and gloom on anyone who crosses their path. For some reason they believe that being a good Christian means never loving anything, that enjoying anything is bad. Have you ever met anyone like that? I find it a very sad spirituality indeed.

Deliver me from people who enjoy being miserable for God! He didn't make you to be miserable and to enjoy nothing. But God does mean for you to grow in purity of heart, to move from lesser goods to greater goods, from lesser holiness to greater holiness. He does mean for you to give up sin and to replace it in your life and soul with good things that you love and cherish, and then to willingly surrender even these goods when he calls for them.

Don't ever listen to anyone who tells you that spirituality is a matter of loving *nothing but God*. Rather, it is a matter of loving *everything in God*. Every saint possesses one reality in common: a great heart. The rest of us suffer from coronary disease of a spiritual nature, with hearts all clogged and cluttered with the junk we've accumulated along the way. Some of it is bad; some is no longer useful; some is just unrelated to the pure love of God.

Through the gift of understanding, the Holy Spirit slowly brings us to the heights of wisdom. We begin to realize that at the end of the spiritual journey, everything begins to converge. Detachment and surrender come together with the riches of faith and the joy of hope. Success or failure, health or sickness, living or dying, all start to move in a single direction. Every aspect of our existence begins to be pulled toward a single reality—God's love calling to us and our being able to respond.

Here is a question that gets to the root of the matter. When you lose something that is irreplaceable and that you really cherish, how do you respond? For example, if you have ever lost someone who was strong and supportive, for whom you could find no substitute, whose absence made you lonelier with each passing day, how did you respond? With anger? Depression? Frenzied activity? Withdrawal? These responses are spontaneous, and only rarely could they be considered "wrong." But neither do they often represent the best spiritual insights into suffering and loss.

If you want to grow in purity of heart, try not to rebel against the hand of God. At times of sorrow and loss, try to perceive with your spiritual eyes the presence of God around you. In losing those things that you cherish the most, you will be most able to grow toward God. And when you know that you can find God even in the losing, then you will have nothing to fear. That is what it means to have a pure heart.

What are the best, the most perfect, the most worthy, the most valuable goods that a human being can possess in this life? Strong, loving relationships with other people. A rich person without any friends or lovers is desperately poor, while a poor person who loves and is loved in return is unbelievably rich.

First Corinthians 13 tells us that if we possess all power, have all faith, and sacrifice all that we have, but have not love, we gain nothing. Everything else is imperfect and doomed to pass away, except love. Yet doesn't even this greatest good seem terribly fragile at times? Don't we suffer the loss of love again and again during the course of our lifetime?

When you lose a close friend—whether it be to death, distance, or discord—the pain cuts to your deepest being. If you have had to bid your parents goodbye, even if they lived to a ripe old age, you know how much it hurts. If you have lost a beloved spouse or a child, you know how excruciating such farewells can be. The pain seems to grow day by day rather than diminish. Even after several months, it never disappears but is merely replaced by a dull ache deep inside.

Yet as Christians, we know that nothing of this sort of goodness has been lost forever. We know that we shall find our loved ones again beyond the grave. That is why everything we do in life should relate in some way to that best of human goods, which is loving relationships. But we have to be willing to sacrifice even those most precious goods when the time comes.

Jesus, the lover of the Father and the lover of souls, will show us the way.

## THE PURE OF HEART SHALL SEE GOD

This last Beatitude of the unitive way sums up the whole challenge of the spiritual life, which culminates in that mysterious pinnacle of human accomplishment: seeing God. Don't be surprised if you feel like you haven't arrived. To some extent we will always see through a glass darkly on this side of the grave. I suspect that most of us are still far from the apex of the spiritual ladder, the realm of the contemplative soul.

But neither should we give up hope, for this Beatitude

promises an astounding reward to the pure in heart: an ever-lasting and loving gaze on the mystery of divine being, the very source of life and of love. Such is the final goal of human life and the eternal resting place of the spirit.

Only once in my life—long ago when I was just eighteen—was I privileged to witness this gaze on the face of a human being, someone who seemed to be seeing God. Overcome with astonishment, I knelt by the side door of our novitiate chapel and watched Fr. Solanus Casey. This humble servant of God was wrapped in ecstasy in the early hours of the morning, his gaze riveted on the tabernacle. I had no doubt that the request that Moses had made was being fulfilled before my eyes: "O Lord, I long to see your face."

Jesus promises us, "I will not leave you desolate; I will come to you.... On that day you will know that I am in my Father, and you in me, and I in you" (Jn 14:18, 20). According to St. Augustine, the call to love God and our sisters and brothers in the world can be accomplished only by being united with Christ—by his birth, by his life and suffering, by his death and all that he does. We must be consistently growing in purity of heart if we are going to truly love others, if we are going to peacefully surrender them when the time comes, and if we are going to eventually enjoy the vision that is the loving presence of God.

Once we have begun to love others with a truly unselfish love, then—and really *only* then—are we approaching some real love of God. We must love the giver and not his gifts. These gifts are many and precious and delightful as they draw us on to God. And the advanced contemplative soul experiences the most wonderful blessings to which the human heart could aspire. But however precious these blessings may be, they must not clutter up the heart.

To realize this Beatitude's promise of seeing God requires that nothing be in the way. This is the utter poverty of St. Francis and the absolute *nada* or "nothing" of St. John of the Cross. Purity of heart leads inevitably to a kind of emptiness, an imagined poverty that can fill us with so much fear in the earlier stages of our spiritual journey. The poet Francis Thompson wrote of this fear in "The Hound of Heaven": "I feared that having Thee, I would have nought else beside."[7]

As we struggle to make progress at the beginning of our journey, we need some assurance that when we get to these higher mountain passages, we will have something, or even better, *someone* to hold on to. An experienced and sincere Christian will tell us immediately what we must cling to: the cross of Christ, our only hope.

The paradox of the cross may leave us more puzzled than pacified. The Messiah seems for a moment to have lost touch with the Father when he says, "Why have you forsaken me?" Then in the next breath he utters the words of final surrender, "Into thy hands I commend my Spirit." The apparent loss of God is the way to finding him. This is not just a nice thought. Keep it clearly in mind, because most probably you will need to remind yourself of this fact in the face of grave illness or death itself.

The Christian soul approaching Calvary needs all the support it can get. Our Savior himself found some measure of support in "the holy women" of Jerusalem and Galilee. He found it in his mother and his beloved disciple, as well as in the other women at the foot of the cross. In our lifelong struggle to really love God with a pure heart, we can hold onto these friends as well. Like Christ, we can find one of the greatest sources of support in the faithful, loving Mother who stood immersed in grief at the foot of the cross.

## CHRIST WILL DO IT

The Beatitudes will be our sure guide on this spiritual journey. Even better, our constant companion will be the just man of whom they speak, Jesus himself. As we abide in him, our struggles and efforts will enable Christ to do his work in us.

Grace is never cheap, of course. And so it is our responsibility to correspond gradually to the grace of Christ and to follow patiently the way of the Beatitudes, to persevere even in the darkest nights and the most painful trials. As we do so, we will begin to understand a profound mystery: that our individual spiritual lives are another unfolding of the passion, death, and resurrection of Jesus Christ.

The following shining paragraph written by the Blessed Edith Stein fits the entire spiritual journey of the Christian into the redemptive act of Christ:

In the passion and death of Christ, our sins have been devoured by fire. If we accept that by faith, and if we accept the whole Christ in faithful self-giving, that is to say by choosing and walking in the way of the imitation of Christ, then he will lead us "through the passion and Cross to the glory of the Resurrection." It is exactly this that is experienced in contemplation: the passing through the atoning fire to the blissful union of love.[8]

It is Christ alone who saves us, and who by his grace leads us on. He alone unlocks the door of eternal life at the end of our earthly journey. He alone purifies us of all sin, that we might approach the throne of God and become fully united with him and with our brothers and sisters for all eternity. And Christ alone makes it possible for us to approach heaven even in this life. He will help us, even now, to begin to hold heaven in our hands.

~

## To Jesus Christ, the Blessed One

*Blessed are you, Lord Jesus Christ, blessed are you! For you are blessedness itself coming from the endless day of eternity and living among us in the passing day of time. Our minds have no way of comprehending what it meant for you "to empty yourself and take on the form of a slave,"* but for our salvation you, the eternal Word, did just that. You came among us to give blessings and you were cursed, to heal and you were wounded, to lift up and you were thrown down, to make peace and you were crucified. What heavenly secret, what mystery lies behind your acceptance of death! It is more mysterious to me that you who are life itself should die, than that you should rise and live eternally, for after all you came here from a place where there is no death but only a fountain of life. It is more of a mystery that the Blessed One should be cursed and crucified than that he should rise and be glorified. But so great was your meekness that it overcame all the strength of evil. So great even now is the humility of God that it defeats the frightening power of evil.

We, O Lord, do not comprehend the passing but awesome power of evil in the world. We see its wrath unleashed at Calvary and at Auschwitz, and in so many places recalled for the evil done there. We struggle with evil in our own lives. We even fight it in our own hearts.

And you, O Blessed One, you are our captain in this battle, our champion in an otherwise hopeless fight. Send your Holy Spirit upon us to give us the weapons to fight on to a victory we could not hope for without you. Write your Beatitudes in our hearts and minds that we may fight on peacefully as you, O Prince of Peace, fought. And may we not be fainthearted or cowardly and may we not shirk and hold back when we are called into battle. But rather, armed with the weapons of peace and justice, may we follow you no matter what it costs. For only then will your kingdom come. Amen.

# Notes

## ONE
### The Way of the Blessed

1. John XXIII, *Journal of a Soul* (New York: McGraw-Hill, 1965), Geoffrey Chapman Ltd.
2. William Barclay, *The Gospel of St. Matthew* (Philadelphia: Westminster, 1975), 88-90.
3. Susan M. Muto, *Blessings That Make Us Be* (Petersham, Mass.: Saint Bede's Publications, 1982), xii-xvi. This entire work can be read with great profit.
4. Katherine Burton, *Sorrow Built a Bridge* (New York: Longmans, Green & Co., 1937).
5. Nathaniel Hawthorne, *Tales and Sketches* (New York: Viking Press, undated), 1068.
6. Omer Engelbert, *The Hero of Molokai*, trans. Crawford (Boston: St. Paul, 1977), 307-30. Also cf. John Farrow, *Damien the Leper* (New York: Sheed and Ward, 1937).
7. Barclay, *The Gospel of St. Matthew*, 94.

## TWO
### Written on Our Hearts

1. John Meier, *The Vision of Matthew* (New York: Paulist, 1978), 6-15.
2. Meier, 62-66.
3. Meier, 42-43.
4. Joachim Jeremias, *The Sermon on the Mount* (Philadelphia: Fortress, 1963), 34-35.
5. Meier, 264.
6. John Henry Newman, *The Heart of Newman* (London: Burns & Oates, 1963), 173. Quotation taken from *Plain Sermons IV*, 243-5, 251.
7. Francis Thompson, *Poetical Works*, edited by Wilfred Meynell (London:

Burns & Oates, 1913) also Modern Library edition (New York: Modern Library, 1969), 349.
8. St. Augustine, *The Lord's Sermon on the Mount*. Ancient Christian Writers, trans. John J. Jepson, S.S. (New York: Newman Press, 1948), now published by Paulist Press, Mahway, New Jersey.
9. St. Augustine, *Sermon on the Mount,* 19.
10. St. Augustine, *Sermon on the Mount,* 220.
11. St. Augustine, *Sermon on the Mount,* 8.

## THREE
### *The First Beatitude of Purification: Cleansing Tears*

1. St. Augustine, *Confessions*, trans. F.J. Sheed (London: Sheed & Ward, 1944), IX, xii, 162-63.
2. St. Augustine, *Confessions*, IX, xiii, 163-64.

## FOUR
### *The Second Beatitude of Purification: Hounded for the Kingdom*

1. Dag Hammarskjöld, *Markings,* trans. L. Sjoberg and W.H. Auden (New York: Alfred A. Knopf, 1965), 149.
2. St. Augustine, *Sermon on the Mount,* 20.
3. Benedict Groeschel and T. Weber, *Thy Will Be Done* (New York: Alba House, 1990), cf. chapter 10.
4. Terence Cardinal Cooke, *These Grace Filled Moments* (New York: Rosemont Press, 1984).

## FIVE
### *The Third Beatitude of Purification: Soul Food*

1. Barclay, *The Gospel of St. Matthew,* 99-102.
2. Andrew Apostoli, *The Gift of God: The Holy Spirit* (New York: Alba House, 1994), 120.
3. Newman, 173. Taken from *Parochial Sermons,* IV, 29.
4. Edith Stein, *Self-Portrait in Letters,* trans. Josephine Koeppel, O.C.D. (Washington, D.C.: ICS Publications, 1993).
5. Patricia Treece, *A Man for Others* (Huntington, Ind.: Our Sunday Visitor, 1982), 98.
6. Archives of Franciscan Handmaids of the Most Pure Heart of Mary, 15 West 124 Street, New York, 10017.

7. Consuela Duffy, *Katharine Drexel* (Philadelphia: P. Reilly, 1946), 268-73.
8. Testimony of Mother Eugenia at the Mother House of the Handmaids of Mary to author, November 1993.

## SIX
### *The First Beatitude of Illumination:*
### *Giving God a Blank Check*

1. Maria del Rey, *Her Name Is Mercy* (New York: Scribner's, 1957).
2. Barclay, *The Gospel of St. Matthew,* 103.
3. William Barclay, *The Beatitudes for Everyman* (New York: Harper & Row, 1963), 68.
4. St. Augustine, *Sermon on the Mount,* 19.
5. Muto, 63-4.
6. Corrie ten Boom, "I'm Still Learning to Forgive," *Guideposts,* November 1972, 3.
7. Ten Boom, 4.
8. George Kosicki, *Now Is the Time for Mercy* (Stockbridge, Mass.: Marian Helpers, 1988).
9. John Paul II, *Dives in Misericordia,* (Boston: St. Paul Editions, 1980).
10. John Paul II, 49.

## SEVEN
### *The Second Beatitude of Illumination:*
### *Second-Class Citizens*

1. Leo Rosten, *The Joys of Yiddish* (New York: McGraw-Hill, 1968), 346.
2. Barclay, *Beatitudes,* 38.
3. David Blumenthal, *Facing the Abusing God* (Louisville: Westminster/John Knox Press, 1993).
4. Blumenthal, 267.
5. St. Augustine, *Sermon on the Mount,* 14.
6. St. Augustine, *Sermon on the Mount,* 19.
7. Mieczyslaw Malinski, *Pope John Paul II* (New York: Crossroad/Seabury, 1979), 91.
8. Malinski, 91-94.

## EIGHT
### *The Third Beatitude of Illumination:*
### *Doing the Work of God*

1. Barclay, *Beatitudes,* 86ff.
2. Barclay, *Beatitudes,* 97.

3. Victor Frankl, *The Doctor and the Soul* (New York: Alfred A. Knopf, 1968), xxi.
4. Muto, 86.
5. Muto, 92.
6. Muto, 91.
7. St. Augustine, *Sermon on the Mount*, 6.


# NINE
## *The First Beatitude of Union with God: The Power of Poverty*

1. Audrey M. Detige, *Henriette Delille, Free Woman of Color* (New Orleans: Sisters of the Holy Family, 1976), 34.
2. Detige, 32.
3. Detige, 13ff. Also see C.B. Rousseve, *The Negro in Louisiana* (New Orleans: Xavier University Press, 1937).
4. Barclay, *Beatitudes,* 20ff.
5. Adrian Van Kaam, C.S.Sp., *Dynamics of Spiritual Self Direction* (Denville, N.J.: Dimension Books, 1976), 179-200 on Self Alienation.
6. St. Augustine, *Sermon on the Mount*, 20.
7. Muto, 106.
8. Thompson, 200.
9. Thompson, 200.


# TEN
## *The Second Beatitude of Union with God: Seeing through a Glass Darkly*

1. Hilda Graef, *The Scholar and the Cross* (Westminster, Md.: Newman Press, 1954), 183.
2. Graef, 229.
3. cf. Barclay, *Beatitudes,* 76-78.
4. St. Augustine, *Sermon on the Mount,* 20.
5. Graef, 229.
6. Edith Stein, *The Collected Works of Edith Stein, Life in a Jewish Family,* Trans. Josephine Koeppel, O.C.D. (copyright 1986 by Washington Province of Discalced Carmelite Friars, Inc. ICS Publications 2131 Lincoln Road NE, Washington, D.C. 20002 USA. Used by permission.), 434.
7. Thompson, 89.
8. Graef, 219.